PRESENTING

Walter Dean Myers

TUSAS 565

Twayne's United States Authors Series
Young Adult Authors

Patricia J. Campbell, General Editor

The Young Adult Authors books seek to meet the
need for critical studies of fiction for young adults.
Each volume examines the life and work of one
author, helping both teachers and readers of young
adult literature to understand better the writers they
have read with such pleasure and fascination.

PRESENTING

Walter Dean Myers

Rudine Sims Bishop

Twayne Publishers • Boston
A Division of G. K. Hall & Co.

Copyright 1991 by G. K. Hall & Co.
All rights reserved.
Published by Twayne Publishers
A division of G. K. Hall & Co.
70 Lincoln Street
Boston, Massachusetts 02111

Photographs kindly provided by Walter Dean Myers.

Copyediting supervised by Barbara Sutton.
Book production by Janet Z. Reynolds.
Typeset by Crane Typesetting Service, West Barnstable,
Massachusetts.

First published 1990.
10 9 8 7 6 5 4 3 2 1

Printed and bound in the United States of America.

Library of Congress Cataloging-in-Publication Data

Bishop, Rudine Sims.
    Presenting Walter Dean Myers / Rudine Sims Bishop.
       p.   cm. — (Twayne's United States authors series. Young
adult authors : 565)
    Includes bibliographical references and index.
    ISBN 0-8057-8214-1
    1. Myers, Walter Dean, 1937–   —Criticism and interpretation.
2. Young adult fiction, American—History and criticism.   I. Title.
II. Series.
PS3563.Y48Z57   1990
813'.54—dc20   90-38062
                                                            CIP

To
JAMES J. BISHOP,
husband and one-man support group,
and
To the memory of his father,
JESSE H. BISHOP, SR.,
1900–1988
Hero to three generations of Bishop men—
and the women who love them.

Contents

Preface

Walter Dean Myers has published thirty-one books for children and young adults in the two decades since the manuscript of *Where Does the Day Go?* was honored by the Council on Interracial Books for Children in 1968. Since 1975, when *Fast Sam, Cool Clyde and Stuff* appeared, Myers has become primarily known as a writer of young adult novels. Of the thirteen novels that are analyzed in this volume, ten have received some official recognition. Several have been cited as a Best Book for Young Adults by the American Library Association or as an ALA Notable Book. Three have won the Coretta Scott King Award, and *Scorpions* was named a Newbery Honor Book in 1989. Myers has become one of today's most important authors of young adult literature.

Myers is a versatile writer; he has produced fiction and nonfiction, books for teenage readers, and books for elementary school youngsters. His importance rests primarily, however, on the quality of his work as an Afro-American novelist. In the mid- to late seventies, Myers, along with Lucille Clifton, Eloise Greenfield, Virginia Hamilton, and Sharon Bell Mathis, was one of the Black writers whose work helped to redefine the predominant images of Blacks presented in books for children and young adults up to that time. They were not the only Black writers publishing in those years, but they were among the most prolific.

Myers's work offers an authentic portrayal of Black urban life. Within the context of a milieu that has the potential to destroy lives, Myers offers love and laughter, compassion and hope, and an emphasis on the spirit and resiliency that enable young people to survive. He also offers humor as a welcome antidote to potential despair.

If Myers's books offer a mirror in which Black readers can see themselves and their lives accurately reflected, they also offer windows or sliding glass doors through which non-Black readers can enter a world different from and yet similar to their own. Myers has become an important writer because he creates books that appeal to young adults from many cultural groups. They appeal because Myers knows and cares about the things that concern his readers and because he creates characters that readers care about and are happy to spend time with. Like all good literature, his books leave the reader with something to think about when the last line has been savored and the book has been closed.

I must begin my acknowledgments by offering heartfelt thanks to Walter Dean Myers for his generosity with time and memories and for his patience with my inquiries and telephone calls. A special thanks to Mr. Myers, his wife, Connie, and their son, Christopher, for offering warm hospitality when I visited their home to interview Mr. Myers in December 1988. All otherwise unattributed quotations and facts throughout this book derive from the tape recordings and notes made during that interview and other conversations.

I am grateful to Amy Cohn, then of *Horn Book*, for recommending me to Patricia Campbell as someone who might write this book. Special thanks are due to Ms. Campbell for acting on that recommendation and particularly for her respectful, supportive, and insightful editing of my manuscript.

Virginia Hamilton was Distinguished Visiting Professor at Ohio State during my writing of the biography chapter, and I thank her and the other members of her writing seminar for a thoughtful reading of that chapter and their encouraging responses.

Chronology

1937	Walter Milton Myers born 12 August in Martinsburg, West Virginia.
1940	Informally adopted by Herbert and Florence Dean. Moves to New York City.
1954	Leaves Stuyvesant High School, joins U.S. Army. Serves three years.
1961	Daughter, Karen, born. Enrolls in writing class with Lajos Egri.
1963	Son Michael Dean born.
1966–1969	Employed as vocational placement supervisor for New York State Employment Service.
1968	*Where Does the Day Go?* manuscript wins first prize in picture book category of Council on Interracial Books for Children Contest.
1969	*Where Does the Day Go?* published.
1970	Becomes senior trade editor for Bobbs-Merrill Co.
1972	With *The Dancers* changes name to Walter Dean Myers. Also *The Dragon Takes a Wife*
1974	Son Christopher born. *Fly, Jimmy, Fly.*
1975	*Fast Sam, Cool Clyde, and Stuff* and *The World of Work.*
1976	*Social Welfare.*

1. Literacy as Liberation: The Making of a Writer

Walter Dean Myers was brought up in a Harlem where little children held hands and sang "Jesus Loves Me" on the way to Sunday school and the streets and parks were safe playgrounds. But his Harlem was also a place where vulnerable and disillusioned young men could easily turn to drugs, gangs, and violence as substitutes for unborn hopes and aborted dreams.

By the time he was a teenager, he was among the disillusioned, but although he flirted with a bit of hooliganism, his major solace—and his saving grace—was reading books and writing stories and poems. Myers was among the fortunate ones. He had been informally adopted by a couple who gave him love and at least two other treasures as well: his mother taught him to read before she sent him to school, and his father told him stories.

Born in Martinsburg, West Virginia, on 12 August 1937, he was originally named Walter Milton Myers. Martinsburg, in the eastern panhandle near Harper's Ferry, was a town of about 15,000.[1] In the mid-1980s, when Myers returned to visit the town with the perspective of urban middle age, he saw it as a tiny place "about twelve blocks long and twelve blocks wide," but at the time of his birth, it was thriving as the only industrial city in the area. In Martinsburg in the late 1930s, however, as in other parts of the country, Afro-Americans were suffering the effects of the Great Depression. Even before the stock market crash of 1929,

Afro-Americans, most of whom held menial jobs on the bottom rungs of the economic ladder, were among the first to be laid off when employers began to tighten their belts. West Virginia was segregated, with separate schools and even separate 4H clubs for "Negroes," and as the rest of the country began to recover from the depression, Afro-Americans had to fight racial discrimination in the job market. One of the many victims of those economic and social conditions was Walter's father, George Ambrose Myers.

Sometime in 1939, when Walter was about two years old, George Myers found himself a widower with eight children and very little means of support. His second wife, Mary Green Myers, Walter's mother, had died giving birth to their daughter Imogene. Among the older daughters were two who had been born to Mr. Myers and a previous wife, Florence.

Florence Brown, part German, part American Indian, had worked with her mother in a German hotel in Martinsburg, and her marriage to a Black man caused her family to ostracize her. That ostracism strained the marriage, which eventually dissolved. Florence initially left her daughters in the custody of their father and moved away from Martinsburg. She later met and married Herbert Dean and by 1939 was living in Harlem. While they were not at all wealthy, they were considerably better off than the Myers family back in Martinsburg.

When Walter was about three years old, Florence and Herbert Dean arrived in Martinsburg to take Florence's two daughters with them to Harlem. But Herbert Dean wanted a boy, and the Deans left Martinsburg with the two girls as well as Walter, who arrived in Harlem "with a snotty nose and wearing a pair of my sister's socks."[2]

The Deans' adoption of Walter was informal, but they became for Walter his "real" parents. He retained no memory of his birth mother and, after the move to Harlem, very little contact with George Myers, although he did maintain contact with his siblings. As a novelist, he writes about surrogate parenting in more than one of his books; it is central to the plot of *Won't Know Til I Get There* and *Me, Mop and the Moondance Kid*.

Walter learned to read when he was four years old. His mother, who sometimes worked in a button factory, taught him to read during the times she worked at home:

> Those were good days. Sitting in that living room, the sun coming through the windows and her starched and ironed curtains. (My mother believed that if you could wash it, you could starch it and you could iron it.) . . . She would do housework. . . . And she would teach me to read. I was about four years old and what we read was *True Romance* magazine. She had an endless supply of *True Romance* magazines. I loved them. I didn't always understand them. I didn't know how these people could get their breasts to heave. Somehow I couldn't get mine to heave at all. She also found some Classic Comics and we went through some of those. This was one of the greatest periods of my life with this woman.[3]

Neither of the Deans had much formal education. Herbert worked as a handyman and shipping clerk for U.S. Radium Corporation. Myers describes him as "small—five foot six, five foot seven. A bull. His strength was like legendary. Carry a trunk full of books down a flight of stairs." Herbert Dean was what his grandson Christopher calls a "manly kind of man." He believed that being a man meant working and feeding one's family and often held more than one job. He worked at the shipyards loading and unloading cargo and at one time worked for a moving company, one of the legitimate businesses run by Dutch Schultz, the notorious gangster and bootlegger of the twenties and thirties.

Herbert Dean left school in third grade and did not learn to read and write until he joined the navy. Walter, however, when sorting through papers after Herbert died, discovered that his father had been barely able to read and write at the time of his death in 1986. That discovery helped explain why Herbert Dean had a difficult time understanding how his son made a living and what kind of man he was. His son was a man who did not go out to work and who made up stories and was paid well for it. Herbert expected that the people who paid Walter would eventually come to their senses or find something else to amuse them and Walter would be forced to find a real job. Nevertheless, it was Herbert Dean who, when Walter was in high school, brought him his first typewriter. Walter remembers that this "manly kind of man" was not afraid to hold his son. When Walter was young, Herbert sat him on his knee and told him stories. Walter remembers the stories as scary ones. "There were stories of ghosts and of rabbits that came through walls and of strange creatures that rose from the sea (the sea was the Hudson River). . . . I was never quite sure I wanted Mama to leave me alone with Herbert."[4] To add to the drama, Herbert acted out some the stories with appropriate sound effects and feigned terror, making Walter's own terror even more delicious.

Apparently the storytelling was a Dean family habit. When Herbert's father came from Baltimore to live with the Deans, he brought with him another supply of stories. Walter remembers his grandfather's stories as " 'God's-gonna-get-you' stories direct from the Old Testament. If I spent too much money on candy, he would relate the story of the man who gave his son talents. If I missed Sunday school, he would tell me about how the Children of Israel had wandered in the desert for forty years because they didn't worship, and any complaint, any complaint whatsoever, I had the entire saga of Job."[5]

Walter went off to school with the ability to read, a head full of stories, and a monumental speech problem. At home, his family seemed to understand his speech. In the neighborhood, his speech was so unusual that when he was a young child, people gave him money to talk. In school, the speech problem led to difficulties. Although he received speech therapy, apparently no one ever diagnosed the problem specifically. Some people suggested that he had a "lazy tongue." a not uncommon diagnosis relating to the speech of Afro-Americans. He was incorrectly diagnosed as having a hearing problem and fitted with a hearing aid. Partly because he could already read at school entrance, his test scores indicated that he was bright, which probably saved him from being diagnosed as mentally slow and tracked in school accordingly. Eventually the problem was, for the most part, outgrown.

Children are not always kind to one another, and Walter's classmates reacted to his speech with laughter and teasing. His response was to lash out and fight his tormentors. His frustration and pride were so fierce that he once threw a book at a teacher whose patience—"Now, boys and girls, just give Walter a chance"—seemed patronizing. He relates that he "did all the things that make a teacher's life a misery, make you pray for snow days in August."[6] Near the end of the fourth grade, the authorities tried to suspend him from school—permanently. A timely attack of appendicitis led to surgery and a medically approved absence for the rest of the term, however, and the next fall he went off to a new school.

Fifth grade was memorable because Mrs. Conway, Walter's teacher, introduced him to literature and to writing: "I had been suspended for fighting in class and had to sit in the back of the class while I waited for my mother to appear. The teacher, known for her meanness, caught me reading a comic under the desk during a math lesson. The teacher decided that if I was going to read then I might as well have something decent to read. Later, she brought to school a selection of books for younger people, and I was introduced to reading good books."[7] The first book from the collection that he read, and the one he remembers as the turning point, was *East of the Sun and West of the Moon*, a collection of Norwegian folk tales.

Mrs. Conway also required students to read in front of the class. Given Walter's speech problems, it was inevitable that he, and the students who dared to laugh at him, would end up in trouble. Recognizing the need for an alternative, Mrs. Conway suggested that he could write something to read. It was the beginning of his writing career. His first attempts were poems written to avoid the *w, r, sh,* and *ch* sounds that gave him difficulty.

In fifth grade he not only was led to good books but discovered the George Bruce Branch of the New York Public Library. Books became his friends. School was misery, even though playing ball in the neighborhood and "running the streets" was a joy. He was, he says, "not much of a social person." He devoured stories because they helped him to cope with the way his life was divided.

Walter grew up on Morningside Avenue in the forties and early fifties. In the neighborhood, especially in the summer, life was pleasant enough. Summer mornings were filled with Bible school and Sunday school; afternoons with basketball in the park, sandlot baseball, stoopball, and Chinese handball. It was a time when adults felt responsible for all the children in their immediate neighborhood, when "anybody could yell at you," and yelling at you was a sign of caring. It was also a time when some famous Afro-Americans still lived in Harlem, and others visited whenever they were in New York. Langston Hughes lived close by. Sugar Ray Robinson the boxer, the original Sugar Ray, came by and "boxed" with the boys on the streets.

Much of Walter's after-school and summer life revolved around the activities available at the corner church, the Church of the Master. James H. Robinson, the pastor, was a progressive minister, taking advantage of the cultural and educational opportunities available in the city and at nearby Columbia University. Operation Crossroads, a church program that sent Amherst College students to Africa, was the precursor to the Peace Corps. Josephine Baker performed at the church. Arthur Mitchell started there what eventually became the Dance Theater of Harlem.

The church also had a gym where Walter and the other boys in the neighborhood learned to play basketball. The gym became the model for the church basement in *Hoops*, where, like Walter and his friends, the boys had flat jump shots because the ceiling was low. The gym was also the setting for neighborhood dances, where the rule was to "leave enough room between you and the girl you are dancing with so that the Holy Ghost could pass through. When the lights were dimmed the Holy Ghost made quite a few detours."[8]

Walter studied modern dance at the church and fondly remembers a production of James Weldon Johnson's poem "The Creation" in which he had the starring role—Adam. His brother, who by that time had come up from Martinsburg to Harlem, played the part of God because he couldn't dance. In this dance production, God simply walked around and surveyed his creations.

In spite of difficulties in school, Walter remembers those years before adolescence as good years, filled with the innocent pursuits of boyhood. Later, when Claud Brown wrote and published *Manchild in the Promised Land*, set in the same neighborhood, Walter did not, he has said, recognize the neighborhood. He was appalled by what he saw as a sensational picture of Harlem as hell, nearly devoid of any love or laughter or the small daily joys and sorrows common to people everywhere. In Myers's early novels—*Fast Sam, Cool Clyde and Stuff, Mojo and the Russians, The Young Landlords*—he recreates something of the Harlem he remembered. Violence, drugs, and crime existed there, but so did basketball and dancing and Bible school at the church.

Adolescence is often turbulent, and Walter's was more turbulent than most. He was placed in an accelerated junior high school program in which seventh and eighth grades were completed in one year. The students in this Special Progress class stayed together for the two years of junior high school, and Walter had what was to be the most successful two years in his school career.

High school was another matter. He was admitted to Stuyvesant High School, which was a boys' school with a reputation for high academic achievement. Its special focus was science, which was not Walter's forte. He had begun to write short stories, some of which were read by Bonnie Liebow. A gifted teacher, Liebow interviewed all of her students and developed an individualized reading list for each of them. "Ms. Liebow made up a reading list for me. I still remember most of the titles—*Buddenbrooks, Pere Goriot, Penguin Island*, something by Zola. I fantasized about marrying her."[9]

Bonnie Liebow not only provided Myers with a reading list but also told him that he was a gifted writer. For the first time he considered the possibility of becoming a writer, though the idea of writing as a full-time profession was still beyond his imagining. His writing also was beginning to bring some recognition outside of school. He won a prize in an essay contest and won an encyclopedia for a long narrative poem. Unfortunately, all of this early writing has been lost.

Bonnie Liebow's attention notwithstanding, Myers spent most of his high school years outside of school. His attendance was so sporadic that one day he showed up for school unaware that it had closed for summer vacation. On days when he was supposed to be in school, he often could be found in Morningside Park, perched in a tree, writing or reading.

Myers worked at various jobs during after-school hours, including delivering packages to the post office for a jewelry business. At the post office he encountered disillusioned Black men who chided him for carrying books, which they interpreted as a sign that he believed he was better than they and that his chances in life better than theirs; he would, they implied, end up exactly as they had. Frightened by the thought that their predictions would be correct, he quit the job as soon as he thought he had earned enough money to buy the typewriter he was working for. He was distressed to discover, however, that it cost more than he had earned. Herbert Dean, recognizing how badly Walter wanted a typewriter, bought him a used Royal office machine. It was a gesture of parental love from a man who saw no practical value in writing stories. Myers used the machine for ten years.

Writing and books offered an escape from a world that Walter perceived as rejecting. Books, along with television and strolls through upper-class Manhattan neighborhoods, also presented different worlds from the one in which he was living. At sixteen he found himself confused, questioning and testing his own changing values against those of his parents and neighborhood. Books, television, and upper-class neighborhoods did not include Blacks in any serious, respectful way. His family did not see any practical value in reading and writing. It was clear that, in spite of his being labeled bright in school, college was not a financial possibility for him. Besides, people in his neighborhood were much more likely to be workers in low-paying, menial jobs than college graduates. For Walter attending college became a dream deferred.

As the Langston Hughes poem of that title reminds us, a dream deferred can have dangerous consequences. In Walter's case, he turned to the life of the streets. He acquired a stiletto, started hanging out with the wrong crowd, skirted the edges of the law, and survived at least one threat to his life. Like Motown, one of the title characters in *Motown and Didi*, Myers dared to intervene in a fight between three gang members and a newcomer in the neighborhood. The gang marked him for death, and one day tried to corner him in the park. He used his stiletto to buy enough space to run to his apartment building where, like Motown, he was safe because the gang knew that they could not easily fight him on the narrow staircases of the building.

It was becoming clear, even to Walter, that he was living a dangerous life. In the mid-fifties, adolescents nearing seventeen and in trouble were often taken to Juvenile Hall and given three choices: straighten up, go to jail, or join the army. Myers joined the army on his seventeenth birthday. He had read Rupert Brooke's poem "Soldier" and been taken with the notion that he might die on some distant battlefield and leave there a little corner that would be forever Harlem.

His career in the army was much less dramatic than he had imagined. He "went to radio repair school and learned nothing about radio repair."[10] Most of his time in the service was spent playing basketball. He also remembers learning "something about killing. I learned something about dying. I learned a lot about facilitating the process, of making it abstract."[11] The attitudes he developed toward war as a consequence of that experience became some of the background for *Fallen Angels*.

Myers spent three years in the army, and in 1957, at age twenty, found himself a veteran, living with his parents in Morristown, New Jersey, and working in a factory. Neither Morristown nor factory work was appealing to him, and he found his way back to New York. In the few years since he had left Harlem, drastic changes had occurred in his neighborhood. Drugs and drug dealers made it an intolerable environment. Myers moved to a cheap hotel on Forty-eighth Street where he rented a room for thirteen dollars a week. It was his "starving artist period," when he lived on unemployment compensation, ate on two dollars per week, lost about fifty pounds, and devoured books.

Eventually, a friend suggested that Myers take the Civil Service Examination. He passed with no difficulty and, like Harry the dragon in *The Dragon Takes a Wife*, "got a good job in the post office." There he met Joyce—six feet, two inches tall, "wonderful,

warm, beautiful, religious, caring."¹² A year later, in 1960, Joyce
and Walter were married, By the end of 1963 they had two children, Karen Elaine and Michael Dean.

After he was married, Walter started writing again, mostly
short stories for adults. These were the heady days of the Black
arts movement, a Black nationalist movement promoting the development of a Black aesthetic distinct from Western literary
traditions. A number of magazines committed to Black writing
were created, and some—*The Liberator, Black Digest, The Black
Scholar, Black World, Black Creation,* and *Essence*—published
Myers's stories. He also wrote poetry, some of which appeared in
Canadian magazines. His first published poem was one written
to his daughter, Karen.

About the time Karen was born, Myers enrolled in a writing
class with Lajos Egri, author of *The Art of Dramatic Writing.* Egri
saw in Myers a special talent and was able to communicate to
Myers his faith that he could become a good writer. Walter found
it difficult to believe that someone who had not gone to college
and had even dropped out of high school could hold his own with
writers with more formal education. But Egri's faith kept him
writing, and he produced a great deal, some of which was published. Eventually, Myers gained enough confidence to recognize
that he had begun writing what he thought the group wanted to
see rather than what his instincts told him he could do best. He
left the group.

The adolescent in turmoil had not yet completely matured. The
job in the post office lasted only a few years, and Myers found
other unsatisfying jobs, such as interoffice messenger in a reha-
bilitation center. In the meantime, he was also trying to live the
life of the bohemian in the East Village—playing bongos, drinking
too much, and as in his high school days, being generally undis-
ciplined. Eventually he and Joyce decided to buy a house in
Queens. Walter, who by then was employed by the New York
State Employment Service, started working two other jobs and
Joyce worked two. But by that time the marriage had suffered
irreparable damage, and within a couple of years they divorced.

Just after the move to Queens, while his marriage was straining

Walter Dean Myers, in U.S. Army uniform, about 1955.

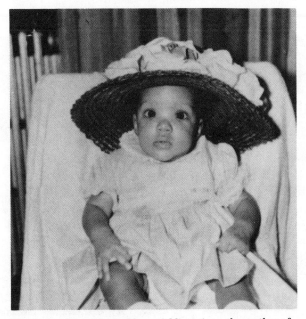

Myer's daughter, Karen Myers Addison (now the mother of three), about 1962.

Myers with Christopher in Hong Kong, about 1976.

Herbert Dean with grandsons Christopher and Michael.

Myers, son Christopher, sister Imogene, wife Connie, sister Ethel.

Michael Dean Myers, U.S. Air Force, 1989.

Myers with eldest grandson, Brandon.

to survive, Myers started attending City College at night. Perhaps stress at home interfered with his ability to study. Perhaps he was haunted by memories of earlier school days. He remembers that college "didn't suit me very much. I couldn't hack that. The only thing I did well in was language. I took French and flunked English." For the second time, he dropped out of school.

Not long afterwards an ad in the *Amsterdam News* led him to enroll in a writer's workshop at Columbia University. It was led by John Oliver Killens, an Afro-American novelist best known for four novels: *Youngblood, And Then We Heard the Thunder, Sippi,* and *The Cotillion.* Killens was also a founder of the Harlem Writers' Guild. Apparently impressed with Myers's talents he recommended that Myers apply for a newly opened editorial position at Bobbs Merrill publishing house. Myers felt anxious about having neither a high school diploma nor a college degree and tried to beg off. But Killens was insistent, and Myers, feeling that Bobbs Merrill should be encouraged in its effort to recruit Black editors, agreed to an interview.

Myers was hired as an acquisitions editor in 1970 and found himself in a new world. The interoffice messenger and civil service worker had become an editor with a large office and a secretary. The dropout who had never been in a large restaurant "soon learned to take a writer or an agent to lunch and spend enough money to feed a family of four for an entire week."[13] The writer who thought that editing meant correcting grammar and punctuation learned to identify promising manuscripts and acquire them for his publishing house. The first book he acquired was the poet Nikki Giovanni's book of prose, *Gemini.*

In the meantime Myers continued writing. In 1968 he had entered the contest for Afro-American writers sponsored by the Council on Interracial Books for Children. The manuscript was the text for a picture book for young children entitled *Where Does the Day Go?* It featured a little Black boy named Steven whose father takes him and an interracial group of children for an evening walk in the park. Steven wonders what causes day and night—where does the day go?—and the children fantasize about the possibilities. Daddy eventually points out that day and night are different, just as people are different: then he explains that day and night are caused by the rotation of the Earth. The manuscript was selected as the first prize winner in the category for three- to six-year-old readers. The next year it was published by Parents' Magazine Press, and Myers's career as a children's book writer was launched.

Myers had entered the contest not because he had a particular interest in writing for children but because he needed to write and this opportunity presented itself. *Where Does the Day Go?* received some criticism for its lack of animation, but generally it was reviewed positively. Its portrayal of a harmonious group of Black, Asian, and Puerto Rican children, accompanied by a father, was especially welcome in the social environment of the late sixties and early seventies.

The success of the first book encouraged others. His second picture book, *The Dancers*, also published by Parents' Magazine Press, appeared in 1972. Michael, a Black child, accompanies his father to his job at a theater and is enchanted by the ballet. He meets a ballerina, who one day drives to Michael's neighborhood with her partner and a musician. She performs on the street for the neighborhood children, and Michael invites her to his house for dinner. After dinner Michael and his friend Karen teach the ballerina one of their favorite dances, the chicken. A few weeks later the children attend the theater to see a performance of the ballet. The book was praised for the freshness of the plot idea and for its gender-neutral attitude toward boys and ballet but criticized for its lack of credibility.

With this second book Myers found a way to pay tribute to the foster parents who had taken him in as a little boy and loved him through a very trying adolescence and a fairly unstable young adulthood. He changed his pen name from Walter Milton Myers, his birth name, to Walter Dean Myers, in honor of Walter and Florence Dean.

It also may be a tribute to Herbert Dean that the featured parent in the first two picture books is the father. At a time when many books about Afro-Americans presented fatherless families, both books portrayed positive interactions between fathers and sons. In his first few adolescent novels, Myers continued to explore, in somewhat greater depth, father-son relationships.

Myers's first two picture books also introduce a second theme that becomes important in his adolescent novels—the importance of the peer group. The interracial group featured in *Where Does the Day Go?* is echoed in *Fast Sam, Cool Clyde and Stuff,* in which relationships among teenage companions are essential. Friends and the support they provide are also important in *The Young Landlords* and *Mojo and the Russians.*

His third picture book, also published in 1972, was the cause of some delight and much controversy. *The Dragon Takes a Wife* was published by Myers's employer, Bobbs Merrill. It features an inept dragon named Harry and a hip Black fairy named Mabel Mae Jones, who greets Harry on their initial meeting with "What's bugging you Baby?" Harry needs to defeat the knight in order to win a wife. After several failed magical schemes, Mabel Mae turns into a dragon in order to show Harry how to move when he fights the knight. Harry falls in love with dragon Mabel Mae, defeats the knight, and gets a good job in the post office, and they live happily ever after. Myers received much hate mail in response to *Dragon.* Some readers were incensed that he tampered with the familiar European folktale by making the fairy Black and having her speak in the street jargon of the day. Others were offended by the portrayal of Mabel Mae, whom they considered to be a negative Black stereotype. Still others objected to legitimizing street language by placing it in a book for young people. The controversy was his baptism by fire into the world of children's book criticism.

Myers continued writing short stories and acquired an agent. His stories appeared in Black magazines, and his articles about bullfighting and other adventures appeared in men's magazines like *Argosy* and *Cavalier.* It was not until 1975 that Myers published his first young adult novel. At a party given by his agent, he met Linda Zuckerman, an editor with Viking. She told him that she had been given the first chapter of his novel and was interested in seeing more. At the time he thought of that first chapter as a completed short story, but when Zuckerman asked for an outline, he quickly produced one, and *Fast Sam, Cool Clyde and Stuff,* an episodic novel that re-creates the kind of Harlem neighborhood in which Myers grew up, was on its way.

Two years after the publication of *Fast Sam,* after a dispute with a company vice president, Myers was fired from his job at Bobbs Merrill. It was 1977, the year he turned forty. By this time, he had married Constance Brendel and they had a young son, Christopher. Karen and Michael were in school, and he had responsibilities for their support. Though his financial obligations made the decision risky, Myers decided not to seek other employment and to become a full-time writer. In his seven years at Bobbs Merrill he felt he had learned enough about the business side of publishing to avoid many pitfalls and earn a decent living. Besides, he had six months of unemployment insurance as a backup.

It was the right decision. In the twelve years since he became a full-time writer, Myers has published thirteen young adult novels, two picture books, and an assortment of others—mystery and adventure books, easy-to-read books, and a novel that invites readers to write their own chapter endings. Although he readily admits that the quality of his work has been uneven, the best of Myers's work has received high praise. In 1988, for example, he published two important novels, *Scorpions* and *Fallen Angels.* *Scorpions* was a Newbery Honor Book, and *Fallen Angels* won the Coretta Scott King Award, both from the American Library Association.

When he became a professional writer, Myers had to define for himself what constituted a day's work. Writers do not punch time clocks, and much of their work occurs in their heads and not on paper. He defined work in terms of a visible product. "I have to have some kind of a job. So I said, 'What's work? Eight hours a day.' I'm sitting around thinking about writing. Am I writing now? Is this work? And finally I got to the point where I said if I do ten pages, that's work."

Myers works at the modest home he shares with Connie and Christopher in Jersey City, New Jersey. He produces his ten pages a day in a small workroom crowded with bookshelves and two word processors. It once was Christopher's room and is still decorated with light blue wallpaper covered with airplanes. Myers, at six feet two and a half inches tall and 210 pounds, nearly fills the space himself. He makes it clear that he loves his work and often has three or four different projects in various stages of completion at any one time. When asked what he does to relax, Myers replies, "Write. If I'm working on something and I feel like that day's over, I may write something else for fun."

With prodding, he confesses that he also plays the flute and has tried the guitar and the saxophone. Another means of relaxation for Myers is travel. Currently many of his trips are related to speaking engagements, but he also has traveled extensively with his sons. He and Michael toured Europe in 1974 and 1975, when Michael was twelve and thirteen. He and Connie and, later, Christopher have visited Asia, Mexico, and South America. His trip to Peru with Christopher provided the backdrop for his mystery-adventure novel *The Nicholas Factor*. A journey to Northern Africa may have provided some background for *The Legend of Tarik*; in any case, the Black knight Tarik furnished the name for the black cat with large yellow eyes who regally resides at the Myers home, ignoring Walter and visitors alike.

Just as his growing up and his travels have supplied background for his novels, Langston Hughes and James Baldwin have supplied inspiration. Their writings demonstrated to Myers that the neighborhood in which he grew up and the people who lived there were rich sources of stories. Hughes and Baldwin freed Myers from his early desire to imitate the European writers he read when he was shunning the public schools and educating himself. Following the lead of Hughes and Baldwin also led him into the perils and pleasures of being defined as a Black writer.

On the one hand he writes of having "an obligation to use my abilities to fill a void."[14] He recognizes the two major problems that have troubled books about Black life in this country: the small quantity of such books, which forces each one to be criticized as if it represents all of Black life, and the historical prevalence of negative images, which makes Black readers especially sensitive to the possibility of insult. He writes of good literature for

Black children as literature that "celebrates their life and their person. It upholds and gives special place to their humanity."[15] He implies that, like Baldwin and Hughes, he wishes to create that kind of literature.

On the other hand, he chafes under the limitations imposed on Black writers by editors and publishers who are unable to accept that a Black writer may be able to write well on topics other than Black life. He also laments that there are so few Black editors in publishing houses that publishers are unfamiliar with Black-related topics, such as Kwanzaa, an Afro-American celebration that occurs during the Christmas season. Publishers who lack familiarity with a topic are likely to reject it as a subject for a book.

In general, however, middle age finds Myers busy and contented, a very youthful grandfather, enjoying his life, enjoying his work. He clearly delights in his children. Michael graduated from the University of New Mexico and has enlisted in the U.S. Air Force. Karen is married and the mother of his three grandchildren. Christopher, who is at home, is tall like his father, outgoing, and full of charm. Just as Myers used his own life as background for some of his early novels, he has used some of Chris's experiences for some of his later books. The idea for *Me, Mop and the Moondance Kid*, which centers on a baseball team, came when Chris was playing baseball. *Mr. Monkey and the Gotcha Bird*, a folklike humorous picture book, grew out of a story told to amuse Christopher on a long trip. The little boy whose father sat him on his knee and told him stories has passed the gift on to his own son.

Myers also shares his gift with other children. He teaches a writing course to a group of sixth-, seventh-, and eighth-grade students at a Jersey City school. He is a serious teacher, pacing back and forth at the front of the library where the group meets, offering some fairly formal and structured assignments and exercises, but his humor is never very far from the surface. The students, most of whom have not had much writing experience, are glad to see him, and some are eager to share their stories. He keeps his criticism gentle but insists that students attempt to improve. It is clear that he enjoys his work with the students. He recognizes what a difference literacy can make in their lives and wishes he could work with more young people.

As he has grown older, Myers has placed a high value on the gift of stories and reading that the Deans gave to him as a child. In his final, successful, attempt to complete his formal education and earn a degree, Myers enrolled in Empire State College, an institution that gives academic credit for life experiences as well as course work. For one of his classes, Myers interviewed a number of prisoners in various penal institutions in New Jersey. He sought initially to understand why these people had "gone bad." He soon recognized that their lives had, in many ways, not been very different from his own. He then began to wonder what had made the difference, what had given him "the strength to turn away from disaster."[16] He concluded that there were two factors that made the difference: First, he had access to reading, which he sees as the "entree into the fullness of society."[17] Second, he had some sense of an ideal for which to strive, some sense of the possibilities available to him in life. For these gifts, he is grateful to Herbert and Florence Dean and to teachers like Mrs. Conway and Bonnie Liebow who passed on the gift of literacy and whose care and nurturing ensured that any experience he was to have in prison would be as "an interviewer instead of an interviewee."[18]

2. With Love and Laughter: Myers the Humorist

Heaven arms with love and laughter those it does not wish to see destroyed.[1]

Just as Walter Dean Myers was no stranger to the potential for destruction and despair among urban Black youth, he was also no stranger to love and laughter as antidotes to despair. Four of his novels—*Fast Sam, Cool Clyde, and Stuff, Mojo and the Russians, The Young Landlords*, and *Won't Know Till I Get There*— portray groups of young people growing up in Harlem, filling their summers and after-school hours with ball games and with adventures and misadventures dreamed up during conversations on the stoop. The books are humorous, but with the humor they also address some serious issues and themes—death, drugs, sex, family relationships, individual and group responsibility.

Soon after he started writing for children, Myers became aware of the serious lack of books about Afro-American children and their life experiences. One of his goals was to help fill that void. The four love and laughter novels succeed not only in reflecting Black urban experiences but also in capturing the rhetoric, the humor, the pain, and the playfulness of young Blacks growing up in a Harlem of a more innocent time.

Their appeal, however, is not limited to Afro-American readers. What connects with young adult readers, regardless of their cultural or ethnic affiliation, is Myers's portrayal of the youth group as a human support system. Group members tease each other, but they also share laughter and tears and rescue each other from the perils of the city and the snares of adults. Further, each of the first-person narrators addresses readers with such honesty and forthrightness that he, if not quite all his tales and escapades, becomes entirely believable and readers feel that they have been invited to become members of the group.

Fast Sam, Cool Clyde, and Stuff

The first of the love and laughter novels, and Myers's first young adult novel, was *Fast Sam, Cool Clyde, and Stuff*, which was cited as an American Library Association Notable Book. It is episodic, consisting of a prologue, an epilogue, and thirteen loosely connected stories. The stories are eighteen-year-old Francis/Stuff's nostalgic reminiscences of the times he and some of his friends experienced after he moved to 116th Street when he was twelve and a half. It is a book about the meaning of friendship and the importance of feelings. Like the other three, it is fast moving and dramatic.

The prologue introduces the three title characters and Gloria, who becomes one of Stuff's best friends. On his second or third day in the new neighborhood, Francis appears on the stoop and is immediately questioned about his abilities. Can he play ball? Can he stuff the basketball? Wanting to meet the challenge, Francis, although he and the group know he is much too short to dunk a basketball, replies that he can if he gets a running start. He has earned his nickname, Stuff, and with a bit more conversation and a basketball initiation the next day in the park, he has become a member of the 116th Street group.

"Miracles of Modern Science" describes Stuff's first escapade with his new friends. In a fight over a girl, Robin, a boy from another block, bites off part of the ear of Binky, one of the 116th

Street group. Enter modern science. Clyde remembers reading in the *New York Times* that doctors successfully reattached a severed finger, and the group decides that the same procedure can be followed with Binky's ear. Paced by Fast Sam carrying the tissue-wrapped piece of ear in his pocket, the kids from Stuff's block run pell-mell into the hospital emergency room, all trying to tell the story at the same time. Someone on the staff calls the police, who arrest all the kids for "disturbing the peace, rioting, and everything else they could think about." When calm finally is restored, the kids explain themselves, the doctor informs them that the reattachment surgery will not work in this case, and they are released. Stuff, in retrospect, sees their sharing of the experience of being arrested as the beginning of their friendship.

Beneath the humor of this episode, Myers reminds readers of the often not-so-funny relationships between the police and the Afro-American community. It is also a statement about the tendency of non-Blacks to assume that groups of Black teenagers mean trouble. When several noisy, excited, but unarmed Black teenagers burst into a hospital emergency room, the doctors and the police automatically assume they are looking for drugs. The police "started cracking heads and dragging us out of there. . . . They made us roll up our sleeves and stuff to check out whether we were junkies or anything."

The same issues are central in the ironic "There's People and Then There's People," in which the three boys are accused of purse-snatching when in reality they chased off the thieves and rescued a stolen handbag. The police assume the boys are guilty, even before the purse owner mistakenly identifies them as the thieves. (She later said the thieves "looked just like" the boys, a reference to the tendency of some whites to declare that all Blacks look alike.) The police officers handle the boys roughly, will not listen to their story, and make no attempt to call their parents. In this case the boys are rescued by witnesses who saw their false arrest and were willing to take the time to travel to the police station and right a wrong. Stuff recognizes the irony in the situation: "So the second thing that got me in jail, besides modern science, was helping people. You get into jail for some very funny things." Through it all, however, Stuff, and presumably Myers, is optimistic. When Stuff's father cynically tells him that he is learning what the world is all about, Stuff rejects the generalization on the strength of his knowledge of many people who are not like the purse owner.

Other incidents are mostly funny. For example, when none of the girls is available or acceptable as Sam's partner in a dance contest, the boys decide to have Clyde dress up as "Claudette." The scheme almost works; they win the contest but have to forfeit the prize when Clyde angrily defends himself against an overly amorous dance partner.

Some incidents have a serious tone. The boys invite Gloria, who brings along Maria and BeBe, to a discussion of sex. Their talk is frank and honest, and the girls help the boys understand the need for mutual respect. They conclude that the decision to be sexually active carries with it a parallel decision to take responsibility for all potential consequences. In a small lapse, the scene begins at Stuff's house but somehow ends, without the characters moving, at Clyde's.

A few episodes are sobering. Clyde's father is killed in an industrial accident. Gloria's father, frustrated by his inability to find work, abandons his family, leaving Gloria withdrawn and depressed. Remembering the support he had received from Sam and Stuff when his father died, Clyde suggests that the group form a club, the 116th Street Good People, to "protect each other, not from fighting and that kind of thing, but just from being alone when things get messed up." When Clyde becomes discouraged because his teachers and counselors imply that he does not have the academic ability to succeed in college, the Good People are there to encourage him. They are also there to help Clyde's sister Kitty cope with her distress over her mother's dating. They even try to rescue Carnation Charley from his own drug addiction and the almost inevitable consequences.

Stuff is, in some ways, the prototypical protagonist for the four novels: bright, easygoing, perceptive, likable. He is a gentle, sensitive young man who describes himself as "kind of scary. If something happens that's a little scary, then you know I'm one of the people that's going to get scared. And I cry easy, too." Typical of people his age, he wants to know that he is not alone in the emotions he experiences. He also displays a self-deprecating humor, an ability to laugh at himself, that endears him to the reader. The incident in which he describes his "being unfaithful to" Kitty (he has not even told Kitty that he likes her) by soul kissing Susan and then fracturing his foot trying to impress her with his karate skills is one of the funnier ones in the book. By the last chapter, he has acquired a number of insights about life and living and particularly about close friendships.

In this first novel, Myers has created a group of memorable characters. Although the episodic nature of the plot and the first-person point of view limit in some ways the extent to which most of the main characters can be seen to change, they are all rounded and individualized. Cool Clyde is not always cool, Fast Sam is not simply athletic, and Gloria is highly vulnerable beneath her hard shell. They all grow in their ability to understand and respect each others' feelings and in their willingness to express their emotions and accept support.

The critical reception of *Fast Sam* was generally positive, recognizing immediately what would come to be known as some of Myers's major strengths: his humor and his ability to create narrative and dialogue that are natural and unaffected. *Horn Book* declared that "the humorous and ironic elements of the plot give the book the flavor of a Harlem *Tom Sawyer* or *Penrod.* . . . The style has the merit of being swift in narrative and natural and vivid in dialogue."[2] On the other hand, Robert Lipsyte cited a lack of dramatic tension. Writing in the *New York Times*, he reviewed *Fast Sam* along with Bethancourt's *New York Too Far from Tampa Blues* and found that both books were "warm and smoothly written. . . . Stuff and Tom are both congenial companions and shrewd commentators of the world around them. But their stories are not compelling. Their authors love them far too much, and we sense early that nothing bad can happen to them."[3]

More typical of the reviews is the one from *Booklist*, which contrasts *Fast Sam* with an earlier, harsher urban novel. "Though a tinge of self-consciousness occasionally marks the otherwise unaffected telling, the string of humorous and sobering incidents that comprise the narrative is engrossing and infused with dramatic impact. Most appealing is Myers' portrayal of tender feelings among friends and his positive acknowledgment of adolescent pain, laughter, mischief and wonder, minus the hard edges in McCannon's comparable *Peaches*."[4]

Mojo and the Russians

Like *Fast Sam, Mojo and the Russians* is also built on some of Myers's remembered experiences. Myers relates that he had an aunt who believed in voodoo or mojo. She once frightened him by sprinkling flour around her door to see whether ghosts would leave footprints. At one time, acting as a marriage broker, she married off Myers's cousin Sterling to a Brazilian woman. When Sterling's affections strayed, "the woman put a pot on the stove, boiled up a blend of spices and herbs, and dropped his picture into it."[5] When Sterling became ill, he decided to stop straying. Myers also remembers that staff from the Russian embassy or consulate were frequently seen visiting the Harlem shops where the accouterments of voodoo were sold.

From these two elements comes a very funny novel about a group of young people who inadvertently become involved with mojo and the Russians. This is a slightly younger group than the one in *Fast Sam*, and the book can be enjoyed by preteens as well as young adults. Various reviewers list it as suitable for grade five through high school.

The affair begins when Dean (Michael Dean, after Myers's older son) tries to win a bicycle race with Kitty and accidentally runs into Drusilla, the neighborhood mojo lady, knocking her down and scattering her groceries. Drusilla, in retaliation, promises to "make his tongue split like a lizard's and his eyes to cross." At first, Dean is skeptical about her power to carry out her threat, but at his friend Kwami's insistence and with a little help from Kitty and the others, Dean comes to the conclusion that perhaps he ought to take the threat seriously.

The problem then becomes how to unmojo Dean. One possibility is to whitemail Long Willie, who is Drusilla's sweetheart. (Kwami insists that one cannot blackmail Black people.) If they can get something on Willie, he will be forced to intercede with Drusilla on Dean's behalf. Long Willie works as a porter at the nearby college. One of his jobs is to shred papers that, he boasts to the kids, are top secret files related to a new weapons system. The other mysterious thing about Willie is that Russians in limousines have been visiting him at his apartment—obviously spies. This calls for "Operation Brother Bad."

The kids divide into subgroups to carry out their operation. One group is assigned to get evidence that Willie is spying for the Russians. Another follows the Russians to confirm their nationality. When their initial plans are foiled, they decide, since Leslie knows a little about mojo, to try some of their own. They start with trying to mojo Judy's dog and eventually decide to mojo the Russian consulate. In the end, everyone turns out to be innocent, the kids do a favor for the Russians, and the reader has been well entertained.

The book is farcical, filled with broad humor and improbable happenings. The escapades the kids get into and narrowly get out of, and the situations in which they find themselves are often laugh-out-loud funny. One of the funniest scenes is the one in which the kids decide to "subliminal" Willie—that is, use an intercom, a borrowed tape recorder, and hidden speakers to give Long Willie a subliminal suggestion. The idea is to convince him that people know about his spying, setting him up to be whitemailed. When they play the tape, recorded at different speeds to achieve a ghostly effect, to the unsuspecting and sleeping Willie, he is genuinely spooked. He runs out of his apartment wearing his bathrobe and causes a riotous neighborhood commotion with his shouts about voices in his room. "Half the block stayed awake for the rest of the night, trading theories about why Willie was running around half naked."

From time to time Dean's first-person narration is interrupted by a change of point of view. A third-person narrator reports on what is happening to Drusilla, mostly through conversations between Drusilla and her black cat, Mama Doc. (Myers has named the cat after Papa Doc Duvalier, former dictator of Haiti, where voodoo thrives.) Through these conversations, we learn what the adults are really up to, which of course has nothing to do with spying or secret weapons. Myers uses the change in point of view and narrative voice to provide the reader with information that could not be known by Dean. It is an effective way to overcome one of the potential limitations of first-person narration.

Although this book is mostly for laughs, it does present, as does *Fast Sam*, a group of believable characters who are loyal to each other and protect each other from interfering adults. One of the characters we get to know best is Kwami. He, like Gloria in *Fast Sam*, is a verbally adroit instigator, and we get to know him largely through his talk. He is the catalyst for much of the action. Like Gloria, he seems to have a fairly brittle exterior, but he shows his vulnerability on at least one occasion. When Kwami, unaware that his mother has been hospitalized, informs his father that he is going to clean his room, his father badgers him with a barrage of sarcasm, implying that his mother's illness was entirely Kwami's fault since chest pains had struck while she was cleaning Kwami's room. Kwami is able to share his pain with the group, which listens respectfully, but minutes later he is back to his usual self, teasing Dean unmercifully about his bungled attempt to ask Kitty to be his girl.

Judy, the white girl from Riverside Drive who hangs out with the group, is an interesting minor character. She becomes accepted as part of the group because she is Kitty's friend. She also becomes the vehicle for introducing the idea that the racist attitudes of adults can poison their children if the children are not vigilant. Judy's parents do not want her to spend so much time in Harlem. Her father, on seeing Kwami's picture on her wall, is upset and declares that he doesn't want any kinky-headed grandchildren. His attitude is mirrored by Kwami's father's anger over Kwami's display of a poster of the bionic woman on his wall. During one of their investigations in Long Willie's apartments, Judy becomes temporarily immobile and two of the boys carry her into Leslie's apartment. When police officers respond to a report that a white girl has been forcibly carried into a building by three Black males, Judy and Kitty insist that the only white female in the room is Kitty, who is, of course, Black.

Dean is in many ways like Stuff—bright, likeable, easygoing, and "scary"—although Wayne is the one who is most timid. Dean's narrative is limited to a description of action and dialogue, and he is defined mostly by his actions. He demonstrates responsibility and courage when he goes alone to Drusilla's apartment to apologize for the accident and later when he spies on a mojo session Drusilla puts on for the Russians. Like the other protagonists, he is just an ordinary city kid pulling off, with the help of his friends, one caper after another.

Even when reviewers found the kids' capers improbable, they praised the humor, the characters, and the warmth of their friendships. *The Bulletin of the Center for Children's Books* found that "The plot is far-fetched, but the gang is marvelous: they tease each other and squabble, but they present a united front to the adult world, and there's a great deal of affection and loyalty and humor in their relationships with each other."[6]

As with *Fast Sam*, the success of *Mojo and the Russians* can be attributed to Myers's ability to create funny situations and believable characters, as well as his ear for dialogue. Robert Unsworth, reviewing for *School Library Journal*, wrote that "Successful fiction for laughs is always rare but twice now Myers has brought in a winner: he has a good ear for dialogue and a real flair for handling funny situations."[7]

The Young Landlords

The Young Landlords grew out of an idea Myers had when he decided he needed larger living quarters and considered buying one of the old buildings being sold for as little as twenty-five dollars by the City of New York. He rejected the idea because of the considerable investment needed to make such a place livable. But he wondered what might happen if teenagers bought such a building. His speculations became *The Young Landlords*.

The Young Landlords is set in the same 122nd Street neighborhood as *Mojo and the Russians*. The group this time is older; all of them are around fifteen. Although the book is certainly funny, it is also a story with a serious theme. Paul, in the end, tells us that "I learned to accept the idea that answers were a lot easier to come by when you stood across the street from the problem. What was harder to accept was that there weren't good answers to every problem, and when there weren't good answers you had to make do the best you could."

Gloria, goaded by the local numbers runner who lectures them at the Numbers Runners Barbecue about wasting their lives, decides that they should do something good. She, Paul, Dean, Omar, Bubba, and Jeannie become the Action Group. On Gloria's list of projects for the group to tackle, just after world peace and cleaning up the vacant lot, is to do something about the Joint, 356 West 122nd Street, officially named the Stratford Arms. The Joint is the neighborhood eyesore, badly neglected, and in desperate need of repair. They confront its owner, Mr. Harley, who abandons the building by selling it to Paul for one dollar. Thus, the Action Group becomes the Young Landlords.

As the teenagers try to find solutions to the difficulties of running a tenement, many of their problems, and much of the humor of the book, come from the eccentricities of their tenants. One of the funniest is Askia Ben Kenobi, a mystic who wears a hooded robe and uses karate to intimidate the landlords. Askia Ben Kenobi arrives at the young landlords' rent party (partygoers pay admission, which helps pay the rent) covered with sacred palm oil, which may well be Crisco, and wearing only a turban, little gold shorts, and a cape. Miss Robinson throws the cheese dip at him, and the party turns into a free-for-all. Net profit—$4.30.

Petey Darden lives in the basement rent free in return for performing the duties of handy man and janitor. He also keeps a still in the basement, which explodes before he can dismantle it and leads to a citation for the landlords.

Mrs. Brown, an elderly woman, believes that Jack Johnson, the first Black man to become heavyweight boxing champion, lives in her apartment. Although Johnson died in 1946, he dies again about once a month, and Mrs. Brown has to be consoled. Apparently he is always resurrected or she is unable to remember his death, so the landlords are periodically called to sit with her while she mourns. The young people are unfailingly compassionate.

Another eccentric character is Mr. Pender, the accountant the landlords hire to keep the books and act as a front for people who will not believe that teenagers can be landlords. Mr. Pender, who was "very short and very neat," looked like an ad for tea, or a Black Charlie Chaplin. He has an investment firm called Financial Banana and takes his leave with a "Peerio! Chip, chip, peerio!" that Gloria, Paul, and Bubba find extremely funny. However, he is a capable accountant, gives good advice, and does not take a salary.

Not all the tenants provide opportunities for laughs. When Ella Fox, the mother of a small child, falls four months behind on her rent, Paul wants to play business man and evict her because the landlords' finances are in poor condition. Gloria angrily argues for compassion and reminds him that the Action Group was formed to do good for people and not put them on the street. In Ella Fox they confront a real world problem for which there are no easy answers.

Some of the humor comes from the situations in which the young people find themselves. Paul and Gloria, who are becoming more than friends, try to repair Miss Robinson's bathroom door but get themselves locked into the bathroom. While they are waiting for Miss Robinson to return to let them out. Gloria has to use the toilet. She insists that Paul turn out the light and unscrew the bulb, which he promptly drops and breaks. Miss Robinson returns at the worst possible moment and wrongly assumes that hanky-panky is going on in her bathroom.

A subplot involves one of their friends, who has been accused of stealing stereo equipment from the store where he worked. Members of the group believe in his innocence, and they have several adventures, including being shot at, as they attempt to find the real thieves. In another touch of reality, when the case is resolved, Chris is not totally innocent, although he has not stolen the equipment.

The conclusion finds the landlords surviving staggering winter fuel bills and managing a second building owned by the Captain, the numbers runner who lectured them at the barbecue. Paul is not certain whether he would buy the building again if he knew what managing it would be like, but he thinks that "Mostly, the whole experience was an up kind of thing."

Once again, Myers has created a believable, likable group of characters who are warm, affectionate, and supportive of each other. Paul, though older, is similar to Stuff and to the other narrators—an ordinary young man who is learning something about life and what it means to grow up Black in the city. Paul, too, is perceptive, has a wry sense of humor, and can laugh at himself. Like *Fast Sam*, *Landlords* offers more than simply humor, and Paul, like Stuff, offers readers insights about people and situations. Over the summer of the story, Paul matures into a responsible young man who learns that solutions to problems are not always clearly black and white.

Myers also touches on a number of social issues that arise in urban neighborhoods, the most common being landlord-tenant relationships, illustrated by the tenants' comments when the young landlords make their initial visit to their new building. Some issues are approached with humor, such as the episode in which Black revolutionaries protest in front of the Joint, yelling about slumlords and oppression until they discover that there is not enough light on their side of the street for the television cameras and the protest moves across the street. Paul wonders how much history is made that way. Myers also points to the casual manner in which the police deal with crime in poor neighborhoods. When the group discovers the stolen stereos, they cannot get a policeman to take a look until Miss Robinson causes a disturbance. Once again, as in *Fast Sam, Cool Clyde and Stuff*. innocent young people are arrested by cynical police officers and handled with unnecessary roughness.

Landlords was the second of Myers's ALA Notable Books, but the praise of some reviewers was tempered by attention to the book's shortcomings. Patricia Lee Gauch thought the book was "a neighborhood block party!"[8] She appreciated the humor and the eccentric characters, but she also found that "the plot . . . stretches the imagination at more than one point."[9] *Kirkus*, while praising Myers's dialogue and "street corner savvy," was even stronger in its concern about credibility: "The whole thing is a little hard to credit."[10]

Generally, however, critics agreed that *The Young Landlords* displayed some of the same talents Myers demonstrated in *Fast Sam* and *Mojo*. The *Booklist* review states, "If the message is serious, its delivery is wrapped in sharp comedy. A unique array of tenants are [sic] skillfully exploited for laughs; ditto for several of the kids' maintenance efforts. Underlying everything is a genuine warmth: these entrepreneurs are a likeable bunch whose trial by fire offers food for thought between chuckles."[11]

Won't Know Till I Get There

Publishers Weekly described *Won't Know Till I Get There*, the fourth of Myers's love and laughter novels, as "another winning novel, told with the nimble wit and poignancy that distinguish Myers's earlier books ("The Young Landlords," "Fast Sam, Cool Clyde, and Snuff" [sic], etc.) about likeable Harlem boys and girls."[12] This one weaves together two themes. One involves relationships within a family, particularly between Stephen Perry, age fourteen, and Earl Goins, the foster child with whom his "good doing" parents have decided to share their home. The other theme, intergenerational conflicts, is developed when Steve, Earl, and two of their friends try to get along with a group of senior citizens.

When Stephen's parents inform him that they plan to adopt a child, Stephen pictures a cute little brother who will follow him around and look up to him. Instead, his parents choose thirteen-year-old Earl, who is five feet five and a half inches tall, one hundred twenty-five pounds, and has a criminal record, including an armed robbery. When Earl arrives, he is not exactly friendly.

Nevertheless, Stephen tries to make Earl comfortable. He introduces him to his friends Hi-Note and Patty. On their way to the basketball court, they go through a train yard. A handy can of spray paint, an unfinished graffito, and the need to impress Earl inspire Stephen to paint on the side of a train "Royal Visigoths," the name of the gang he would have when and if he ever organized one. When they are questioned by transit police, Patty and Hi-Note join in the bragging about the nonexistent gang, and all four youngsters are arrested. As restitution for their crime, they are assigned to work at the Micheaux House for Senior Citizens for the summer.

The seniors are a feisty group, healthy and fiercely protective of their independence. The city is closing the home, and they must either find enough money to run it themselves or find places to live. They do not welcome the teenagers or their aid, since they do not wish to be seen as helpless. They insist on being called "seniors" and not "elderly." It takes time and several confrontations for the old people and the teens to begin to understand each other, trust each other, and accept each other's help.

At home, Earl's presence causes some soul searching and conflicts within Stephen's family. As Steve struggles with his own feelings about Earl and gradually comes to understand why Earl is prickly, his parents feel that their plan is not working the way they had hoped. They had expected that adopting a troubled child would make them feel good about themselves and possibly engender gratitude from the child. Instead, Earl doesn't get along with Steve, gets into trouble at the Micheaux House, and adds tension to their home. The decision to return Earl to a social service agency at the end of his trial period causes a row between Stephen and his father. Eventually, his parents' concerns are alleviated, and the family makes plans to adopt Earl. This leads to the brief introduction of Earl's mother, who cannot bring herself to permit her son to be legally adopted. She does allow the Perrys to become his legal guardians until he is eighteen, however, at which point he can make his own decision.

Myers again uses a first-person narrator. This time the story is related as Stephen's diary, addressed "To Whom It May Concern" (TWIMC, or Twimsy). The voice is honest, forthright, and funny. When his parents tell him that they are planning to share their good life with another child, he asks if they are going to have a baby. His father replies, "Not exactly, son." Stephen writes, "It was definitely heavy. They were going to have a kid, but not exactly. The last time I saw somebody not exactly have a kid she had to leave school anyway." Much of the humor in the book comes from such comments from Stephen and from the dialogue that he records and reports.

As with the other love and laughter novels, some of the humor also comes from situations and escapades. Myers has a knack for creating funny visual images. When Steve and Earl prepare dinner as a surprise for Steve's parents, they decide to cook something unusual so they cannot be criticized for not knowing how to cook even the simplest thing. They buy frozen octopus, but as the octopus thaws, its legs fall into place, making it look very much like a live creature staring at them from the kitchen counter. They scoop it into a plastic bag, but when Earl opens the door for Steve to run to the trash can, Steve runs directly into his father. "He snatched the bag from me and looked in it. Dude jumped about thirty feet straight up. He dropped the bag and everything. I never knew my father could curse like that. . . . Earl was lying on the floor laughing. . . . Even after the Kentucky Fried Chicken had been delivered and everything explained, my father was still mad."

By the end of the book, Steve and Earl have become "brothers," and the Perry family has been strengthened. The seniors, however, even with the help of the teenagers, have not been successful in their efforts to save their home. The boys and Patty are disappointed by the callousness of the social agencies that are responsible for the elderly. Although three old people have found satisfactory places to live, one is lonely in a nursing home and another is on the street. The love and laughter are mixed with a taste of bitter herbs as Stephen and his friends realize that people need to be accepted as the individuals they are; they cannot be defined by categories or labels.

The critical reception of *Won't Know* was similar to that of the other three love and laughter novels. The major negative criticism was a certain didacticism found in the conversations between the residents of the home and the teens. Except for her assessment of the plot, Hazel Rochman's review is typical: "In spite of the creaking plot, readers as always, will love the dialogue, the fierce and funny repartee and the grotesque insults; and also the masterly control of dramatic scenes: the way in which bantering explodes into violent hostility, the move from slapstick to pathos, the sudden stabs of psychological insight. The overt didacticism is quite superfluous: excellent characterization clearly demonstrates Myers' theme."[13]

Common Threads

The love and laughter novels offer a mixture of reality and humor. The city is a backdrop, but it is not an oppressive environment that becomes a negative force in the lives of young people. If these books offer a message, it is that growing up Black in the inner city doesn't automatically equate with being downtrodden and impoverished. Within that environment, kids will be kids, having good fun and sharing with their rural and suburban agemates the same emotions and concerns.

Myers also places a high value on peer groups and the support they can provide for members. In these books the peer groups are small communities. The focus on finding strength in community which arises from a shared sense of Blacks as an oppressed people, is common in young adult novels by Black writers. Some of Myers's groups are, however, racially integrated. *Fast Sam* has some of the few positive Puerto Rican characters found in books of the period. *Won't Know Till I Get There* even has an interracial marriage. *Won't Know* actually features two groups, the teenagers and the seniors. The old people value the friendships they have forged, and one of the plot problems is how they all can manage to stay together. Myers also is concerned about the status of females as members of the community. All of Myers's groups include girls and nonsexual friendships between males and females. The girls are generally strong characters who can hold their own with the boys. Kitty is faster on her bike than almost all the boys in *Mojo*, and Gloria is a respected basketball player in *Fast Sam*.

For the young people, the group is a place to try out some of their ideas about what it means to be a man or woman in their time and place.

Myers has a habit of using the same names for different characters. In some instances, it arises from fatherly affection: characters carry the names of his children, Karen, Michael Dean, and Chris. There is a Gloria in *Fast Sam* and another in *Young Landlords*. A girl named Kitty shows up in two of the novels. Minor characters also share names with minor characters from other novels. When asked about his choice of names, Myers said that he tends to associate certain names with certain characteristics. A girl who is tough and who will not stand for any nonsense is a "Gloria." It may be, then, that not only the male protagonists, but other characters in the love and laughter novels are prototypical Myers characters. For anyone who reads more than one of the novels, keeping track can be confusing, as evidenced by the reviewer who had Paul, in *Landlords*, in love with Kitty, who does not appear in the book. Paul has a romance with Gloria.

Fathers and Sons

In each of the four love and laughter novels, the relationship between the narrator and his father is an important thread. Mothers are positive and supportive, but mostly they are stock characters; the boys are trying to understand their relationship with their fathers, all of whom seem to have achieved some measure of success after overcoming odds. They are determined to see that their boys are well brought up and that they "make something of themselves." Their characteristic method for doing this is to lecture their sons periodically. Dean, Stuff, and Stephen all report that their fathers lecture to them—about world events, how they should spend their time, or how much more privileged the sons are than their fathers. Often, the fathers resort to sarcasm, which can be hurtful, as is the case with Kwami. On the other hand, when Paul's father uses sarcasm to remind him to pick up his own trash, Paul is annoyed but recognizes that his father is right.

With the possible exception of *Mojo and the Russians*, in which the group is fairly young and the focus is on the plot, the father-son relationships are on the way to being resolved by the end of the book. The sons recognize that although their fathers may have difficulty expressing their emotions verbally, they genuinely love their sons and want the best for them.

The fathers, however, are not always inarticulate about their feelings. When Stuff is on his way to the police station to be questioned in the case involving Carnation Charlie, his father puts his arm around him and assures him of his support. Stephen's father, knowing his son's concerns about Earl usurping his place, tells Steve he loves him.

The interactions between the fathers and their sons sometimes do not advance the plot but offer insights into character. For example, in *Mojo* the confrontation between Kwami and his father helps us to know Kwami better, but since *Mojo* is a plot-centered book, and neither theme nor character growth is a central concern, it is a somewhat isolated incident.

There is a chapter in *The Young Landlords* in which Paul accompanies his father to Martinsburg, West Virginia (where Myers was born) for the funeral of Mr. Williams's brother. Their conversation in the car on the way down gives Paul some insight into his father; on the way back Paul is able to help ease his father's pain. Again, the scene has enabled us to know Paul and his father better but has little to do with the two plot lines: the running of the Joint and the clearing of their friend's name. In this book, however, the relationship between Paul and his father is a minor theme, part of Paul's growing up, along with his developing sense of the complexities involved in trying to solve social problems.

In focusing on these relationships, Myers does two things. He shows glimpses of his male protagonists having a typical adolescent experience, such as working through conflicts with their fathers on their way to becoming independent young men. He also offers his readers images of the Black male as father. The fathers of Stuff, Dean, Paul, and Stephen are also Myers prototypes. They are not perfect: they do not always say the right things, and their lecturing may be ineffective. But unlike Black fathers in many urban novels of the seventies, these fathers have not abandoned their families; they are working to support them. They care about what their sons are doing, they do their best to instill their values in their sons, and when the chips are down, they are there to provide support and guidance. They offer some glimpses into what it means to become a Black man and a responsible and loving parent. They represent Myers's version of the everyday kind of hero.

Black Vernacular and Black Rhetoric

Critics unfailingly acknowledge Myers's ear for natural-sounding dialogue as one of his major strengths. In the four love and laughter novels in particular, much of the flavor and authenticity of the dialogue and much of the humor emanate from Myers's ability to capture the flavor of typical oral discourse among urban Black adolescents. Part of what Myers so accurately records is the way young men, especially, use their skill with words as a way to establish their masculinity and to establish their superiority over those less skilled.

This verbal sparring or showing off is rooted in the oral traditions that are a major aspect of Black language and culture. Afro-American novelists, working within both a literary and an oral tradition, have historically used aspects of Black vernacular to enhance their art. Myers is no exception. He uses the grammar, the semantics, and the rhetorical styles of Black English vernacular to full advantage, both as part of the dialogue and as part of the style of narration.

It is important to an understanding of Myers's work to examine the way he uses Black language patterns to sharpen the focus on his characters and to add levels and layers of meanings that enrich his novels and place them within the tradition of Afro-American novels in general. One of the best sources of information about Black English is Geneva Smitherman's *Talkin and Testifyin: The Language of Black America*.[14] Smitherman is a linguist who teaches at Michigan State University. Her book is a comprehensive description of the linguistic elements and the rhetorical styles that define Black English. The following discussion draws heavily on her work.

In the first episode of *Fast Sam, Cool Clyde and Stuff*, Myers introduces the notion of signifying, one of the four modes of discourse identified by Smitherman as important aspects of Black language use. Smitherman defines signification as "the verbal art of insult in which a speaker humorously puts down, talks about, needles—that is, signifies on—the listener."[15] According to Smitherman, signifying has a ritualistic aspect, and knowlegeable participants conform to certain rules.[16]

In *Fast Sam*, when Robin and a couple of his boys come by to pick a fight with Binky, Robin starts with a false accusation that Binky had been talking about him behind his back. Gloria, eager to see the fight, starts signifying: " 'You know, Binky, I think you were wrong,' Gloria went on. 'Robin looks like a nice cat. I don't believe half those things you said about his mama.' 'Say what? What you say about my mama, man?' Robin's scar was twitching and the veins started standing out on his neck."

Gloria's signifying intends something other than the literal meaning of her words. Her intent is not to correct Binky's misperceptions about Robin and his mother, but to "put on" Robin, to make him angry so that the boys will fight. Robin does not recognize, or chooses not to acknowledge, that Gloria is signifying, not reporting truth. So he breaks one of the rules of the game; he takes it seriously. In doing so, Robin assumes that Binky has violated another rule—that the person being signified on must be present. Signifying is not done behind one's back.

Seeking to avoid the fight, Binky tries at first to persuade Robin that he should not accept Gloria's signifying at face value and that he, Binky, never said anything about Robin's mother. Robin, however, takes the denial as a sign of weakness and bans Binky from his territory on 118th Street. Binky has now been placed in an untenable position in front of his group. He comes back with a verbal signal that he is willing to take Robin on: "Look Robin, I don't want to argue with you. I believe in equal opportunity for people who've been in terrible accidents, and from the way you look, I can see your face has been in just about the most terrible accident I've ever seen."

In implying that Binky has been talking about Robin's mother, Gloria also introduces one of the better known forms of signification—the dozens. The dozens involves insulting a person's nearest relatives, particularly a person's mother.[17] Insulting one's mother is a sure-fire way to make a person angry—unless it is done in the context of the ritualistic playing of the dozens and follows the rules, one of which is that there can be no element of truth in the insults. In traditional form, the dozens frequently refer to the mother's sexuality or to various sexual acts performed with her or other close female relatives, hence the dirty dozens.[18]

In *Won't Know Till I Get There*, Earl engages in the dozens in one of his exchanges with Hi-Note. When Earl takes a cue from the seniors and starts lecturing the other young people about their not knowing what it is like to be old, the following exchange occurs:

> "Well how you know?" Hi-Note said.
> "I just know," Earl said.
> "Well, *how* you know, turkey?" Hi-Note stopped right in front of Earl. "How long you been old?"
> "Since I been running around with your mama!" Earl said in a mean voice.

In the opening scene of *The Young Landlords*, Gloria signifies on the numbers runner, known as the Captain. The fattest person at the Numbers Runners Barbecue, he is eating while some of the young people are running races: "Anyway, Gloria saw him sitting there and had to go open her mouth. 'Hey, Captain,' she said, 'how come you ain't out there running in the races? You might win first prize!' "

Gloria does not directly refer to the Captain's size or to the fact that he is engaging in his favorite pasttime—eating—nor does she directly suggest that he could use some exercise. However, all those meanings are implied in her signifying.

The Captain's response is not to laugh but to answer with a brief lecture that demonstrates another rhetorical strategy steeped in the Black oral tradition. Smitherman labels this strategy tonal semantics—the use of rhyme, voice rhythm, repetition, alliteration, or tone to give meaning to one's utterance or to simply make it sound good.[19] Here, the Captain uses repetition of the nothing theme and the repeated sentence structure to make his point that the young people are wasting their lives:

> "I don't understand about you young people anyway," the Captain went on. "You been to school and you don't know nothing, you got you a little bit of money and you ain't got nothing, got your whole life in front of you and you ain't going to nothing."
> "What I do comes from not being able to do nothing better. What you do is 'cause you don't want to do better."

The Young Landlords provides an example of still another mode of discourse steeped in the oral tradition of Black culture, the use of call-response patterns. Although this mode is probably most frequently associated with the church, it also is used in secular settings. It is a communication process in which a speaker and his or her audience interact. The speaker's statements are responded to with verbal or nonverbal expressions from the listeners.[20] Among Myers's male characters, the most frequent form of the call-response mode is the nonverbal "giving five," the slapping of hands. In *The Young Landlords*, there is a scene in which a protest group tries to take over the Joint.

> "When I say REV-O-LU-TION I mean just that! REV-O-LU-TION! A revolution is a turn. A wheel turns! A wheel turns and they call it a REV-O-LU-TION! And that's what we are here about! Do you hear me?"
> "Yeah, we listening." . . .
> "Let them on through!" the speaker said. "We ain't got nothing to do that we can't let the world see us! I am an oppressed man seeking to regain my rights! To have the rights that God has given me, and which this oppressive society has taken from me and turned over to the slumlords of the ghetto, the gunlords down in the Pentagon, and the funlords in Atlantic City!"
> "Go on and preach now!" somebody yelled out.
> "Look at this raggedy building that our people are supposed

to live in! Look at the busted-up garbage cans and dirt in front
of it! Is this where our children are supposed to play? *Is it?*
"No!" came back the chorus.
"You bet it ain't! But that's where they got to play! And this
raggedy building is where our people got to live while the fat
landlord lives downtown in a high-rise building and sends his
fat wife to Florida for a suntan!"
"That's the truth!" a woman standing right next to me said.

The fact that the audience is responding with its verbal inter-
jections indicates that the speaker is being effective with his audience. In this setting, if the audience were quiet, the speaker
would be deemed a failure. Note also the use of tonal semantics
in the play with "slumlords, gunlords," and "funlords" and with
the word "revolution." This skill at spontaneous word play is one
of the markers of a successful orator in the Black tradition.

Much of Myers's use of Black vernacular focuses on individual
verbal performances, or raps. Smitherman asserts that in the
Black experience there is a tradition in which "verbal performance
becomes both a way of establishing 'yo rep' [your reputation] as
well as a teaching and socializing force."[21] These raps may display
one or more of several qualities: exaggerated language, mimicry,
the use of proverbs or aphoristic phrasing, punning and word play,
spontaneity and improvisation, image making and metaphor,
braggadocio, indirection, and tonal semantics.[22] In having his
characters make use of almost all those qualities, Myers effectively paints them as acculturated into the Black linguistic and
social tradition.

In *Mojo and the Russians*, Kwami is the character who is the
most adroit rapper and therefore takes a leadership role. From
the opening scene, in which Dean accidentally runs into Drusilla
with his bicycle, Kwami displays his spontaneity and virtuosity
with rhyme. When the policeman tells Dean to be careful so that
he doesn't hit anyone else with his bicycle, Kwami says, "The only
way my man is going to hit anybody else with that bicycle is to
pick it up and throw it at them. . . . He can be trusted 'cause his
machine is busted." As he examines the bike, he declares, " 'You'd
better check yourself out and check yourself steady.' Kwami

slapped his palms together like he was giving himself five—'because that old witch done got you already.' "

Sam, in *Fast Sam, Cool Clyde and Stuff*, provides a good example of braggadocio or boasting. He is demonstrating his prowess as the best dancer in the neighborhood in preparation for the dance contest. Stuff suggests that if he can get Gloria to go with him, he is sure to win.

> If? What you mean *if*? She be a fool not to want to go to a dance with Fast Sam. Because the way I spin she got to win. . . . The way I move she got to groove. . . . I wish I was one of them schizophrenics and had me a split personality. Then I'd say later for Gloria and go to the dance with myself. Now wouldn't that be bad? Out of sight. Gloria, baby, here come Fast Sam to spread the word of joy to you. And Stuff, you be ready to catch her if she pass out.

Gloria is less than overjoyed at the news and provides a verbal performance of her own, one that may be more typical of Black women than men. In any case, it is full of vivid imagery and is improvised on the spot. "You pimply-faced, big-nosed, wide-mouthed, bug-eyed, bad-smelling, pigeon-chested fool! If I got hit by a car you couldn't take *me* to a hospital."

There are numerous examples of word play. For one, there is Kwami's reply, in *Mojo and the Russians*, to Dean's explanation that he has had a slight accident: "Now you got a slight bicycle." There is Jeannie's rejoinder to Omar's assurances that the owner of the Joint in *The Young Landlords* is not likely to send a hit man to get Paul: "He could probably take care of you with a hit *boy*."

There are also numerous examples of image making and the creation of metaphors. In *Mojo and the Russians*, Kwami is skilled at spontaneous imagery. He describes Drusilla as looking like a bad dream. When Dean denies being frightened, Kwami says, "Then how come when I said I saw Drusilla you jumped up so fast you almost left your eyeballs on the stoop?"

Interestingly, much of the image making comes from the character who is the narrator and thus is removed from dialogue and becomes part of Myers's more general narrative style. It is Stuff who describes Cap's look as one "that would turn chocolate milk into sour cream." It is Steve in his diary who describes Earl as "looking like a bad dream at high noon." Dean, the narrator of *Mojo*, describes the Mojo lady, Drusilla's, breath as smelling like a deserted building.

It is likely, too, that what some reviewers see as a lack of credibility in the plots of these humorous novels is in actuality an aspect of Myers's use of Black rhetorical strategies as part of his style. One of the characteristics of effective rappers is that they tend to employ hyperbole as part of their way of telling a story. Just as the readers enjoy a description of the Captain as not smiling except once a year at Christmas, they are expected to enjoy a bit of exaggeration in the description of the incidents the narrator is relating.

Because Myers's narrators are also the protagonists in these books, they remain in character and speak to the reader with the voices of adolescent or preadolescent boys. They, too, employ some of the rhetorical strategies of the other characters, even when they are addressing the reader and therefore including the reader as a member of the group. Thus, Steve, in *Won't Know Till I Get There*, describes for Twimsy his relationship with his best friend, Hi-Note, with the rhyme, rhythm, and metaphor characteristic of a good rap: "Now Hi-Note had been my Main Man. My Ace from Inner Space. My Grit and Spit Brother, My Get Down Partner, A True Believer, My Brother Bad When the Times Were Sad, and the Jamming Trans to my Slamming Fusion."

Both the narrators and the other characters in their conversations make use of the grammar of Black English vernacular, such as the absence of the *be* verb ("He over to his aunt's house"), the multiple negative with inverted auxiliary ("Ain't nobody said nothing"), the apparent absence of the third-person singular *s* on the verb ("It sound a little like Mojo to me"). However, much of the narration also employs standard English grammar or the informal grammar and vocabulary of casual English speech.

Myers makes effective use of what Smitherman calls Black semantics, "the totality of idioms, terms, and expressions that are commonly used by Black Americans." [23] The books are sprinkled with terms—"cool," "jive," "bad," "dig," baby," "heavy"—which are often considered street talk or slang and are therefore perceived negatively. Smitherman points out, however, that the use of these terms is an example of the tendency of Blacks to "appropriate English for themselves and their purposes."[24] Although some of the meanings of the terms are shared by whites and Blacks alike, some meanings are peculiarly Black, such as "bad" to mean "good." Myers also occasionally uses terms such as "doo-rag" (a scarf used by Black men to keep their hairdos in place), which may not be generally known outside Black cultural contexts. Thus, Myers's use of Black semantics is one more strategy by which he establishes and delineates the Black cultural setting of his novels.

In these four books, however, Myers avoids the use of the language usually identified as obscene or foul. There is an occasional "pee," as in "scared the pee out of me," or a "hell," as in one character inviting another to "go to hell," but for the most part, the young people in these books use vocabulary that would be accepted in their homes and schools.

Dual Consciousness: Black Culture and Middle-Class Values

Myers's characters can be recognized as genuine reflections of Black youth growing up in a Black cultural setting. Sprinkled throughout the books are references familiar to Blacks—names such as Jack Johnson and Al Green, experiences such as rent parties and New Orleans funerals, beliefs such as voodoo or being born with a veil over one's face. However, his characters can also be recognized as American middle class. Unlike several of the novels featuring Black characters that were published prior to *Fast Sam*, Myers's love and laughter novels feature intact, middle-class families.

It is not difficult for middle-class readers to see reflections of themselves and their families in these books. The fathers of Stuff, Dean, Paul, and Stephen all have white-collar jobs. Stuff's family has moved into the neighborhood so that Stuff can have his own room. Stephen's parents, both of whom work outside the home, want to share their good fortune with a less fortunate child. They visit the museum frequently enough for Steve to be able to mimic his father's museum lecture. The lectures the fathers sometimes give their sons often have to do with bettering themselves. The group in *Fast Sam* think it is important for Clyde to go to college. In these ways, the boys and their families share the typical American dream.

This dream is shared across social groups, which makes the books accessible to a broad range of readers. Urban Black youth have an opportunity to see themselves and their experiences reflected in a positive, upbeat way, and other readers are offered an opportunity to share in those experiences and in the love and laughter that are such vital aspects of Black life and culture.

3. On Compassion and Hope: Myers the Realist

The Harlem that offers Stuff, Dean, Paul, Stephen, and their friends opportunities for laughter is also a Harlem where social services are often hard to secure, jobs are hard to find, drugs are plentiful, and violence an everyday occurence. In one of his poems Langston Hughes envisions it "on the edge of hell,"[1] but Myers can see the possibility of rescue from the abyss. His viewpoint is essentially an optimistic one. In his realistic urban novels, he often sets his characters against potentially destructive societal conditions so that the inner city itself plays a major role in ways similar to humans-against-nature survival novels. Within that environment, characters are often placed in conflict with their inner selves, struggling to maintain their integrity in the face of nearly overwhelming odds.

The six realistic novels are marked by Myers's sympathetic portrayals of his major characters. His compassion sometimes extends even to those characters whose behaviors we deplore. He may provide a vignette or two from their past that explains, but does not usually excuse, their current behavior, raising for the reader questions about why different people caught in similar circumstances make different choices. The novels are also hopeful. All the protagonists survive and for the most part do so with renewed strength and the promise of a better tomorrow. In his study of the Afro-American novel, Bernard Bell, professor at the

University of Massachusetts, concludes that "the value most frequently celebrated in the tradition of the Afro-American novel is the spiritual resiliency of a people to survive, individually and collectively, with dignity and to realize fully their human potential."[2] Survival is the major theme of these six novels, confirming Myers's membership in the academy of Afro-American novelists.

The novels were published over the decade from 1978 to 1988. Two of them, *It Ain't All for Nothin'*, his first nonhumorous novel, and *Crystal*, published nine years later, portray young people in potentially destructive situations from which they must extricate themselves. *Motown and Didi* is a love story, without much laughter but with the conviction that love can overcome seemingly overwhelming odds. Two others, *Hoops* and a sequel, *The Outside Shot*, explore the notion of basketball as a way out of the inner city and as a metaphor for life. *Scorpions*, a 1989 Newbery Honor Book, portrays a young boy who, like the protagonists of *Crystal* and *It Ain't All for Nothin'*, must extricate himself from a destructive situation. But though he survives. Myers's vision in this book is darker and less optimistic than it was ten years earlier.

Making Choices: *It Ain't All for Nothin'* and *Crystal*

On the surface these two novels are quite different, but they can be examined together as examples of Myers's philosophy of individual free will—that an individual always has choices and the strength to make the right ones comes from within oneself. Tippy, the narrator and protagonist in *It Ain't All for Nothin'*, tells the reader that "I was being two people. I was being me on the outside . . . and then I was being me on the inside. . . . I was thinking that the inside me was the real me." Crystal tells her father, "It was like there were two of me. A real me underneath and an outside me that was pretty and sexy." Both protagonists struggle to listen to their inner selves.

Myers's third novel, *It Ain't All for Nothin'*, was a serious break from the humor of the first two, *Fast Sam* and *Mojo*. Tippy, who is twelve, has been raised by his Grandma Carrie. When she becomes ill and has to enter a nursing home, Tippy reluctantly moves in with his father, Lonnie, who supports himself by petty thievery and spends most of his time drinking and smoking weed with his friends. He has no food in his refrigerator, no routine in his life, and no concept of how to be a father. He sometimes beats Tippy, sometimes gives him money and sends him to the streets, and sometimes offers what he considers fatherly advice. Lonnie also coerces Tippy into taking part in robberies, and although Tippy deplores his participation in the robberies, he is disturbed to discover that they excite him. Feeling "like a dying calf in a thunderstorm." Tippy turns for solace to alcohol and to a bus driver who befriends him and eventually becomes a substitute father. When Bubba, one of Lonnie's friends, is mortally wounded in a robbery, Tippy makes the decision to defy Lonnie and try to save both Bubba's life and, in a psychological sense, his own. He and Mr. Roland, the bus driver, call the police, who arrest Lonnie and his friends.

While Tippy lives on the edge of poverty, sixteen-year-old Crystal, in the novel of that name, is approaching wealth and fame. She is a model who was discovered when a commercial was filmed at her church. Unlike Tippy, Crystal is not alone. She has a mother who is living her own lost dream through Crystal, a father who worries about the potentially negative effects of her career, and an agent who plans to exploit her youth and sexuality. She also has some good friends, particularly Sister Gibbs, her elderly neighbor, and Pat, her high school classmate. Although she wears beautiful clothes, appears in public with famous people, and sees her picture in magazine ads, she also experiences the darker side to the modeling business. Her friend Rowena, a white eighteen-year-old model whose look is no longer in style, commits suicide. Crystal is pressured into posing for a men's sex magazine. A producer expects her to have sex with him in return for a part in his movie. Eventually the stresses become more than she is willing to bear, and she finds the courage to give up modeling to enjoy what is left of a normal adolescence.

Both Tippy and Crystal ultimately return to the values they were brought up with, and Myers explores those values through the Black church. Historically, religion has been important to Black families, both as a source of strength and, in the case of Black churches, a part of a distinctive Black culture. Afro-American novelists have traditionally drawn on the language of the Black church and its music as sources of linguistic style, character delineation, and themes.

Tippy's grandmother is a religious woman who teaches him to pray and to have Christian values. We come to know Grandma Carrie through her prayers, her affirmation of religion as the sustaining force in her life, and her efforts to make Tippy keep religion at the center of his. When Tippy confesses to her that his father is a thief, Grandma Carrie tells him, "Ain't no true Christian person can stand a thief!" In the end, when he is struggling over what to do about the dying Bubba, Tippy tells himself that if he allowed Bubba to die he, Tippy, would bear the major responsibility because "I knew I was not supposed to be this way. I didn't know how Stone and Lonnie was supposed to be." Grandma Carrie had told him that "when you can't reach around and grab nothing to help you. . . , you had to reach inside yourself and find something strong."

Grandma Carrie worships and prays at home, but Crystal is an active member of her church. She sings with the gospel choir, making it easy for Myers to use Black music to make a point. In one of the modeling scenes, when the photographer tells her she is sexy and simply needs to let others see it in her, Crystal is reminded of the contrast with the words of a religious song—"Let Others See Jesus in You." Crystal also has seventy-seven-year-old Sister Gibbs, a neighbor and friend, to help reinforce her values. Sister Gibbs tells her, "You can't read the Bible and not know how to live your life. . . . You just keep on living like you know you supposed to. Don't let nobody turn you around, girl." Like Grandma Carrie, Sister Gibbs is described in part by her speech, which is sprinkled with expressions straight from the church, such as "the devil's handiwork" and "as God is my secret judge."

Crystal and Tippy are both exploited, and exploitation becomes one of the major sources of tension in the novels. Crystal's mother,

Carol, an embittered woman, sees Crystal's modeling as an opportunity to relive her own life, to have a vicarious second chance at the career she gave up for marriage and family. She blames her husband for her lack of a career and is unable to forgive him for robbing her of an opportunity for fame and fortune. Her obsession with Crystal's career makes her unable to be the mother Crystal needs. Unlike Sister Gibbs, she has lost her perspective on right and wrong; in the name of professionalism, she urges Crystal to put up with almost any humiliation or degradation in order to advance her career.

Crystal's agressive agent and the photographers she poses for see her as a beautiful meal ticket. They know that if they can package her as dark and sexy, they can play to the fantasies of large numbers of white males, who will in turn spend money on whatever product is being sold with her image. Loretta, her agent, tells her, "Think of yourself as a feast. Everybody is going to want a part of you." Hers is a fresh face that they will use as long as it promises to bring them money, but Myers's portrayals of the racism, insensitivity, and coldness of most of the people who control the modeling business suggest to the reader that Crystal can easily be replaced by another beautiful young model.

Tippy is exploited by his father and his father's partners in petty crime. Soon after Tippy comes to live with Lonnie, Bubba suggests that Tippy can be Lonnie's ticket to a welfare check. He coaches Lonnie on how to present himself at the welfare office— unemployed, hungry, broke, and illiterate. Lonnie also insists that, just for the duration of the welfare interview, Tippy call him Daddy, an appellation Lonnie had rejected earlier. Tippy is also forced to act as a lookout and, in one instance, a decoy in Lonnie's robberies.

In escaping from the exploitation that threatens them, Tippy and Crystal both have the support of adults outside their families. Surrogate parenting is an important motif for Myers. Himself the beneficiary of such an arrangement, he includes some aspect of surrogate parenting in four of the six realistic novels. In the case of Tippy, Mr. Roland is the bus driver who befriends and in the end gains custody of Tippy. We learn little about Mr. Roland, but his availablity to Tippy is important to the plot. For Crystal it is Sister Gibbs who provides the kind of mothering and advice Crystal's mother is unable to give. In both cases, Myers seems to be celebrating the traditional values of the Black community, which holds that children are the responsibity of all adults.

As in the love and laughter novels, Myers continues to explore the bonds between fathers and their children. The fathers in both *Crystal* and *It Ain't All* are portrayed with compassion. Although Lonnie of *It Ain't All* is far from being a model parent, he is not totally indifferent to fatherhood. He is weak and defeated and has only a vague sense of what it means to be a father, but he does make an effort. In a scene in which the drunken Lonnie tries to play a game of basketball for Tippy's benefit, Myers helps us to feel how much Lonnie missed the presence of a loving father in his own life. In some of the conversations between Tippy and Lonnie, we are given glimpses of Lonnie's unfulfilled dreams and ambitions and, in a particularly tender scene, his love for Tippy's mother, who died in childbirth, and his budding affection for Tippy. He even takes a job and seems to be on the road to changing his life for the better. But he is fired and is convinced to try "just one more" robbery to get a stake to help him change his life.

Tippy wants to find the father in Lonnie. He keeps searching Lonnie's face in an effort to see what he will be like as a man. But as he begins to see Lonnie for what he is, Tippy is distressed to discover that he is beginning not to like Lonnie or the way he looks. Tippy realizes that Lonnie is trapped in his own life and that it is a kind of life that Tippy cannot live. As the book ends, Tippy decides that even though Lonnie has hurt him badly, he still wants them to "be okay" simply because Lonnie is his father. Lonnie acknowledges that Tippy made the right decision in trying to save Bubba, so Tippy dares to hope. The final words in the book are, "I'm still hoping." In the meantime, the kind and caring Mr. Roland and his wife will be the parents he needs to nurture his growth to manhood.

Crystal lives with both parents, but the relationship with her father is the more positive one. Daniel Brown, much like the fathers in the love and laughter novels, talks to his daughter about the things he wants for her. He wants to be able to give her something to help her "get over," to help her be ready to meet the world. He feels "caught between a poor man's dream and a rich man's nightmare and afraid to let either one of them go." Unlike some of the boys' fathers in the love and laughter novels, Daniel is able to articulate his affection for his daughter. When he retells the story of how the joy of her birth had, for him, transformed ordinary icicles into crystals, inspiring her name, we see his love for her. In that same conversation, we hear him wistfully speak of how much his wife used to love him; when Crystal declares that Carol still loves him as much. Carol is unable or unwilling to confirm the statement. Again, Myers gives us, through Daniel's conversations with his wife and daughter, glimpses of the forces that have shaped his life, and we are sympathetic.

Myers makes it more difficult to be sympathetic to Carol Brown as she relates to her husband. Seeing him as the stealer of *her* dreams, she is incapable of nurturing his, or of celebrating his successes. On the other hand, she is a character more to be pitied than hated, and Myers evokes the reader's sympathy with his portrayal of Carol's desperate need for Crystal to become a star. When Crystal tells her mother that she needs a vacation from modeling, Carol is so distressed at the thought of her dream dying once more that she loses control, breaking glasses and hammering her hands against the kitchen wall. Crystal puts her to bed and decides to continue modeling a while longer. When Crystal finally does make the decision to stop modeling, we are left only with Daniel's assurance that Carol will be all right. In the light of her previous behavior and attitudes, that assurance is not convincing.

As in the love and laughter novels, much of what we know about the vividly drawn characters in these two realistic books is revealed through their speech. In introducing us to Sister Gibbs as Crystal fixes her hair, for instance, Myers captures the flavor of the typical chit-chat that goes on among Black women in such situations. He also portrays Sister Gibbs as being quite facile with the kind of imagery that is typical of Black vernacular speech: "They didn't make me with this morning's coffee, you know" or "She didn't say nothing, but she give me one of them looks like to turn hard cheese into buttermilk, like she don't believe a word I'm saying." Other characters speak equally distinctively and believably.

Crystal and *It Ain't All for Nothin'* share similar themes. *Crystal*, however, in spite of the situation in which the main character finds herself, is lighter in mood than *It Ain't All*. Myers shows the negative side of modeling but balances it with the glamour. Crystal is a strong character, and we care about what happens to her. This is not a book about modeling but about Crystal's struggle to maintain her integrity and remain true to herself and her values.

On the other hand, *It Ain't All for Nothin'* is almost unrelentingly grim. Tippy is standing near, if not on, "the edge of hell," and the first-person narration pulls the reader into caring deeply whether he finds the strength to pull himself to safety. When he does, we are relieved and, like Tippy, hopeful. Tippy, too, has made the choice to be true to himself, and we feel he will survive.

Love but Not Laughter:
Motown and Didi: A Love Story

Tippy and Crystal look inside themselves to find the strength they need for their own psychological survival. Motown and Didi must find inner strength, but they also have each other. Their story is one in which love transcends the worst that the mean streets of a drug-infested city can hand them. Motown was a minor character who befriended Tippy in *It Ain't All for Nothin'* and showed him some tricks for surviving on his own on the streets. Didi, just out of high school, feels trapped by her family responsibilities. Her father abandoned his family when she was a child; her brother Tony is a drug user; her mother is neither physically nor mentally well.

Tony's involvement with drugs brings Motown and Didi together and nearly ruins their lives. Angered over her brother's addiction, Didi goes to the police to demand that Touchy, the local supplier who has hooked Tony on heroin, be arrested for dealing drugs. The police simply notify Touchy that she has "dropped a dime" on him, and he sends some of his henchmen to teach her a lesson. They are trying to drag her to a rooftop to beat and rape her when Motown, arriving home and noticing the scuffle down the street, cannot bring himself to ignore it. He attacks the henchmen and she escapes.

Didi wants to thank Motown, and her visit to his home in an abandoned building begins a friendship that blossoms into an unlikely love story. Burdened by her brother's addiction and her mother's instability, Didi wants nothing more than to get away, the farther from the neighborhood the better. She has applied for scholarships at colleges as far away as Eastern Washington University. The last thing she wants or needs is to fall in love with someone like Motown, who seems to have little prospect of doing anything more than trapping her where she is.

Motown is an orphan and a veteran of a string of foster homes. Like Earl Goins in *Won't Know*, he had been taken in by a woman who wanted to supplement her income with the payments given to foster parents by the child welfare agency. As soon as she had saved enough money for a down payment on the house she wanted, she turned him back to the authorities. He is a loner who thinks he is self-sufficient, and he trusts very few people. At his core, however, he has retained the capacity to love. Like Tippy, Motown has a surrogate father, this time in the person of the Professor, who owns a bookstore. He feeds Motown's mind with books and philosophy and worries about how Motown is feeding himself.

Improbable though it may be, and in spite of the young couple's good sense, their love grows like a weed between the cracks of a cement sidewalk. When Tony dies of a drug overdose, Didi demands that Motown kill Touchy for her. This time the Professor rescues both Motown and Didi from possible tragedy. In a chaotic final scene, Didi is injured, Touchy is finally arrested, and Motown and Didi ride off in an ambulance reaffirming their love.

Were it not for the environment in which it flourishes, this might be an unremarkable love story. It is the contrast between the tenderness and sweetness of their love and the harshness of the streets that provides both the tension and the theme. *Motown and Didi* is the first of Myers's urban novels in which he moves away from a first-person narrator. (*Crystal* has a third-person narrator, but it was published later.) He uses an omniscient point of view to provide the details that make the milieu believable and reveal his compassion. We see Touchy, the drug dealer, being psychologically abused as a child by his wife-beating father, and we begin to understand why he is so cold and unfeeling that he doesn't want to be touched. This scene also helps us understand that drug dealing and the things it buys represent for him manhood, which his father has taught him he must not let anyone take away.

Myers is compassionate, but his social conscience permits him neither to absolve Touchy and his henchmen from all blame nor present them as the only villains. Through Touchy's conversations, Myers shows that the drug trade flourishes with the collusion of some police officers and under the direction of people "downtown," outside of Harlem. Mr. Bell, a drug distributor with headquarters on Forty-second Street, refuses to expand Touchy's territory because Touchy has not yet learned to "love money more than the garbage that lives up there." When Touchy weakly defends Harlemites by protesting that only the junkies are garbage, Bell reminds Touchy that he bears responsibility for helping to create the junkies.

Myers's narrator effectively describes action and thoughts from various distances and in various voices. When he is an objective observer, the voice uses standard English. Here is Motown remembering his foster care experience: "On the night that he dreamt these things it had snowed and the wind howled outside the windows of the Institute and rattled the front doors down the long, pale green hall. For some reason, known only to God and the secret voices within him, he had thought . . ." At other times we are both inside and outside the character. When we are observing Tony trying to pull himself together, for instance, the narrator's voice is similar to Tony's, even though it is not dialogue:

"He knew he had to get his head together, that some heavy action was going down. . . . He was right, the stuff was gone. The same sucker that had helped Didi when Touchy's boys were teaching her a lesson." When Tony takes his fatal overdose of drugs, Myers brings us directly into his mind for a heartbreaking look at his final moments.

Tony and his addiction are the catalyst for much of the action. He is a tragic figure, victimized by Touchy, by his own lack of direction, and by the absence of anyone other than Touchy to help him understand how to be a man in his world. Although this is a story about the power of love to overcome formidable odds, even Didi's love cannot save Tony.

Through the Professor's philosophizing, Myers expands his theme beyond romantic love and its power to overcome adversity. Like other Afro-American writers, Myers is concerned about the future of young Blacks; he reminds Black readers of the importance of community. Myers has the Professor tell Motown: "We're all in the tribe from the moment that we're named until the moment that the last memory of our deeds is gone. . . . The tribe has got to have numbers and the strength of each person. . . . When you walk down the street and you see members of the tribe falling by the wayside, you have to understand that that's part of you falling over there." Thus, when Didi wants to know why Motown has helped her brother, he answers, "Cause he's either my people needing help or he ain't." Myers reminds us that the entire community is facing adversity and the entire community needs help.

He also has the Professor remind us of the potentially tragic consequences of forgetting or not knowing one's history. Before we can gather the strength to love others, we must find a way to love ourselves. The Professor laments: "Got no respect for each other, got no love for each other. But what can you expect when you don't even know who you are? You don't know what kind of a people you from? You got to be able to respect yourself before you can respect anybody else." The idea of romantic love, then, is expanded to include love of oneself and love of one's people.

Breaking Out: *Hoops and The Outside Shot*

Tippy, Motown, and Didi have survived and, like many poor city dwellers, will likely find their destiny in the city neighborhoods where they grow up. Crystal chooses to "go home" to Bedford Stuyvesant, but it is clear that she will have other choices when she is ready to make them. For many young Black men in the Harlems of this country, basketball represents the potential avenue to fame and wealth. Few ever become professional ball players, but as long as some do, the dream is kept alive. In *Hoops* and its sequel Myers suggests that, in a few cases, basketball can provide an "outside shot," but that the player must have more than basketball skills to succeed in the game of life. He does not try to kill the dream but to keep the feet of the dreamers planted on the rock of reality.

Within the context of these sports stories Myers continues to explore themes he has introduced elsewhere—friendship, father-son relationships, love. In *Hoops* Lonnie Jackson (same first name as Tippy's father, but a different character) is finishing his senior year and participates in a citywide basketball tournament as he tries to decide what to do with his life. In the sequel, *The Outside Shot*, Lonnie has won a scholarship to a small midwestern college, and we follow him through his freshman basketball season.

Hoops is as much the story of the relationship between Lonnie and Cal Jones as it is about basketball. The friendship gets off to a rocky start but develops into a warm father-son bond. When Cal is introduced as the coach of the team. Lonnie recognizes him as the wino he had encountered lying on the playground basketball court. At first Lonnie refuses to play, but he relents, and the friendship grows as Cal hones the boys' athletic skills and shapes them into a winning team. Lonnie learns that Cal was once a professional basketball player who was expelled from the game because of his involvement in a point-shaving gambling scheme. When it begins to look as if Lonnie's team might win the tournament, local gamblers and sponsors try to see that the team loses. When they try to keep Lonnie out of the championship game, Cal decides to play this final game his own way. When it is over, the team has won with Lonnie's help, but Cal pays for his defiance with his life.

Both books have enough basketball action to satisfy sports fans, and the descriptions of the games are colorful and dramatic enough to engage even the nonfan, but neither is just another sports story. Lonnie is a three-dimensional, dynamic character, and the reader comes to care about his fate. His senior year in high school finds him adrift, uncertain about his future, having difficulty getting along with his mother, and finding in basketball his major source of self-esteem and confidence. In *Hoops* we see him not only on the basketball court but trying to work out a romantic relationship with Mary Ann and to understand the changes in her brother Paul, who had been his good friend. We also see him, of course, trying to understand the changes that are taking place inside himself.

Because he was abandoned long ago by his own father and because basketball is such an important part of his life, Lonnie is ripe for a friendship with an adult who can help him not only with basketball but with growing up. Cal, however, is still engaged in the search for himself, so the building of this pivotal relationship proceeds neither smoothly nor predictably, defining the plot as it progresses.

Lonnie at first finds it difficult to trust Cal, particularly since Cal gives him reason not to. Cal makes a persistent effort to persuade Lonnie to play with the team and take advantage of the opportunity to win a scholarship. But when Lonnie takes the first steps and orders his uniform, Cal fails to show up for a game. When Cal finally appears at the community center, Lonnie's violent reaction is out of proportion to the circumstance. Clearly, more than a game is at stake, as Ox, one of Lonnie's teammates, recognizes early on. "Sound to me like you kind of sweet on the dude. How long this been going on?" Lonnie resorts to playing the dozens for his comeback—"Since I got tired of your mama, sucker"—but it doesn't disguise the fact that he has an emotional investment in the tournament and in Cal.

Lonnie is the narrator, and through his meetings and conversations with Cal and his ex-wife, Aggie, we learn Cal's history.

As the bond between the two men grows, we learn how Cal once succumbed to the temptation of easy money from the gamblers who feed off professional sports. We also find out how difficult it was for Cal, with basketball his only skill, to find suitable work after his expulsion from the game. We see how the pressures of being out of work, out of the spotlight, and in disgrace inevitably affected his marriage. The final break-up came after his son was accidentally killed in a fire when Cal left him in the care of a babysitter while he worked. That he tries to drown his woes in alcohol becomes understandable. Although it is clear that Lonnie has invested his emotions and trust in Cal, Myers keeps the reader in suspense about whether Cal will be able to hold himself together long enough to coach the team through the tournament and justify Lonnie's trust. He disappears for days at a time, missing practices and leaving the team without a coach for two tournament games. Eventually, he decides that, though he has thrown away his own game—in basketball and life—he can help Lonnie have at least an outside chance of keeping his game together. Lonnie represents a second chance for him. He teaches Lonnie what he has learned—that "the game is more than what goes on out on a basketball court" and that after basketball is over, one still has to go on living. Cal's final act is heroic, but Cal is no stock hero. Myers uses Cal's story to make statements about both the promise and the peril of relying on basketball as a ticket out of a poor inner-city neighborhood and into the good life.

Lonnie has concerns other than Cal and basketball: his romance with Mary Ann and the apparent schism in his friendship with her brother, Paul. As Lonnie comes to love and trust Cal, he also begins to be open to the possibility of loving Mary Ann. Since both Lonnie and Mary Ann have difficulty getting along with their mothers, and both have places to stay outside their mothers' homes, it is not surprising that they become sexually involved, although the emphasis is on Lonnie's initial fear of commitment and his gradual growth toward being able to acknowledge and express his feelings. His contact with Cal's ex-wife and his recognition of the depth of the love between Cal and Aggie also provide him insight into the potential joy and pain involved in loving someone.

Mary Ann's brother, Paul, is a relatively minor character who is at the center of a web of connections between Lonnie, Mary Ann, Cal, and Tyrone, the extortionist and gambler who proves to be the major villain. Paul is also the character through whom Myers explores some of the far-reaching and insidious effects of racism. Having once seen his father humiliated by his white bosses, Paul longs to join a Black social class that he feels doesn't have to put up with such assaults on their dignity. He begins to associate with light-skinned, upper-middle-class Lennie, his sister, and his sister's friend, Joni. In order to get money to impress the girls and keep up with their social activities, he stoops to stealing welfare checks, for which he receives fifteen dollars apiece. Continuing to associate with Joni even though he has overheard her say that he and Harlem are only curiosities to her, Paul fails to see that he is losing his own self-respect in order to avoid his father's fate. For him, basketball also represents a potential escape.

Lonnie survives the tournament, but even though he loses Cal, he gains confidence that he can "get his game together" and make something of his life. Cal and basketball have helped him to find the same kind of inner strength that enabled Tippy and Crystal to survive. The tournament has allowed him to be seen by college scouts, and he is hopeful. He knows that he might not make it but that he is "going to give it [his] best shot."

The Outside Shot follows him through his freshman season at Montclare State College in Indiana. The Montclare basketball is somewhat different from the street basketball he knows. As a freshman, he is no longer a star. He finds that he must struggle to keep up academically, and he becomes involved with a lovely Black athlete whom he has trouble understanding. He also discovers that college basketball is no more a squeaky clean enterprise than the pros or the New York tournaments. He must continue to fight racism and the gamblers who want to corrupt the players and the game.

The basic story is simple. Lonnie makes friends with his room-mates, starts a friendship with Sherry, makes the team, and earns money by working with a severely withdrawn little boy. He nearly loses everything when rumors about his involvement in a point-shaving scheme lead to an investigation. In that crisis he is helped and supported by Cal's friend Sweet Man Jones and the Broth-erhood, a group of Black professional players. His innocence is confirmed, and he is ready to get on with doing what is necessary to make the most of his "outside shot."

His closest friend at college is his roommate and teammate Colin, a white farm boy from Cisne, Illinois. Myers does not em-phasize that this is an interracial friendship, but by having Lonnie visit Colin at home, he makes the point that poverty and its effects are experienced by whites living in Middle America as well as inner-city Blacks. Colin's mother is uncomfortable with Lonnie not because he is Black but because he is a college boy, and she fears her lack of formal education will show her to disadvantage. Montclare and basketball are as much Colin's ticket to a better life as they are Lonnie's. Colin is a likeable character and a loyal friend, and Myers makes the friendship believable.

The character who reminds Lonnie and the reader of the peril of not being prepared to cope with life after basketball is Ray, a Black ex-Montclare player who never quite made the pros. Re-flecting on Ray's suicide Lonnie recognizes something of himself in Ray and determines not to give up: "Montclare . . . was a world that had some things in it that I wanted, and . . . I had a slim chance of making it after all. I told myself that I wasn't ever going to give up. . . . If I had an outside shot, I was going to take it."

The different settings, characters, and basic problems make it unnecessary to know the details of *Hoops* in order to understand *Outside Shot*. Readers who start with *Hoops* may be unhappy that the romance with Mary Ann is easily disposed of in the sequel. When Sherry at Montclare asks about his New York girl-friends, Lonnie declares, apparently seriously, that he had played the field and now wishes he had someone back home to write to.

In *Hoops*, however, he declares that "I loved her [Mary Ann] more than anything that I had ever loved before." It is easy to accept that teenage romances don't last forever, but this one was treated seriously in *Hoops*, and it is disappointing to find it expendable in the sequel.

In any case, Sherry, even though she perplexes Lonnie with her on-again, off-again attitudes toward him, does help him to learn to respect her and, by extension, women in general, as individuals and as equals. She is sometimes confused herself, and though she proves to be a good friend, she is a not an altogether convincing character, probably because we see her only through Lonnie's confusion.

Through Lonnie's involvement with emotionally disturbed and withdrawn nine-year-old Eddie Brignole, we see his sensitivity and his compassion. Basketball once more becomes a vehicle, this time for communication and building a bond of trust and affection between Eddie and Lonnie. The relationship with Eddie is also an opportunity for Lonnie to recognize that he has talents beyond basketball. He succeeds with Eddie where others have failed.

In these two books, Myers returns to the first-person narrative voice and to the vernacular of the Black urban adolescent. Here is Lonnie on Ox: "But I knew what he was like when he was mad, stronger than skunk pee and meaner than King Kong's dog, so I left him alone." In addition to offering lifelike dialogue, this voice also allows Myers to return to the humor that is missing from most of the urban reality novels.

These two books appeal to readers who enjoy fast-moving sports stories, but beyond that they have something to say about survival and hope. Lonnie, as much as Tippy in *It Ain't All for Nothin'*, has to "reach inside [himself] and find something strong." As he ends the season at Montclare, he tells us that for the first time in his life he feels he has a good chance to live the way he wants to live. He has learned that "It was about a lot more than playing ball. It was about knowing what was out there, what to go for, and what to walk away from."

On the Edge of Hell: *Scorpions*

There were ten years between the publication of *It Ain't All for Nothin'* and *Scorpions*. Jamal Hicks in Scorpions is twelve, the same age as Tippy, but his Harlem is ten years older and ten steps closer to hell. It is the Harlem of boom boxes, brand-name sneakers, and armed gangs of young boys selling crack on the streets. As Reverend Biggs tells Jamal's mother, "It's a hard life sometimes, Sister Hicks."

A hard life indeed. Jamal Hicks is nearly robbed of his childhood by overwhelming circumstances. His eighteen-year-old brother Randy is in jail for having killed a man in a robbery attempt. His mother, raising her two other children alone, has no money to pay for an appeal. Jamal is urged by Randy's friend Mack to take over his brother's gang, the Scorpions, and earn the money by running crack. Alleging that the takeover is Randy's wish, Mack gives Jamal a gun, and nothing is ever quite the same. The gun provides the illusion of power, but it drives a wedge between Jamal and his best friend, Tito, and inevitably leads to tragedy.

On one level, this is a moving story about the friendship between the two boys. Tito, a Puerto Rican who lives with his grandmother, is a gentle, timid, innocent dreamer living in an environment that does not nurture gentleness or timidity. He follows Jamal's lead, borrows his clothes, and is unfailingly loyal. He is also a conscience for Jamal, the small voice warning about the inevitable consequences of relying on a gun to instill respect and engender fear. Tito is certain that it is wrong to keep the gun and is literally sickened by the burden of having committed, albeit in defense of his friend's life, what he believes to be a mortal sin. His certainty comes, like Tippy's, from the religious upbringing his grandmother has provided.

Jamal, too, possesses gentleness. He likes to draw and does so reasonably well. At home, he takes care of his younger sister, appropriately called Sassy, and worries about his mother and how she will cope with the problems burdening her. Religion is important to Jamal's family, too, although it doesn't seem to provide for him the same sure guide to his behavior that it does for Tito.

Outside his home, even though he has more street smarts than Tito, Jamal is often made to feel "small inside, and weak." Dwayne, the class bully, challenges him at every opportunity. Store owners hurt his pride. Bigger kids laugh at him. Teachers embarrass him in front of the class. The gun, then, represents something larger than himself and makes him feel strong. He realizes that he is wrong to keep the gun, but he also realizes that another part of him does not want to give it up.

His friendship with Tito, then, is one of the few bright spots in Jamal's life. Together they dream of the boats they will buy to take them to Puerto Rico. Together they can simply be the children they still are, sharing with each other their secret desires and their secret fears; they are nearly perfect complements to each other. The friendship is marred by the presence of the gun, however, and because of the fight with the Scorpions Tito has to move to Puerto Rico to live with his father.

On another level this is a story about the difficulty of simply being a respectable human being in an environment in which traditional values are turned upside down—where adults use children to run drugs, where money is more important than human life, where manhood is represented by material possessions, and where violence is a casual means of self-expression. Myers builds the setting detail by detail: the addict nodding against the light pole outside Jamal's window, Jamal restricting Sassy to one piece of chicken so their mother can have supper, the family doing without hot water for days at a time, a man slapping Jamal for leaning against his Mercedes.

This harshness is contrasted with Jamal's times with Tito, the love of the family, and the true-to-life rendering of affectionate brother-sister verbal sparring between Jamal and Sassy:

> "You think you cute or something?"
> "All I know is what I see in the mirror," Sassy said. . . .
> "Mama, she think she cute," Jamal said.
> "She is cute," Mama said.
> "No she ain't."
> "Tito think I'm cute," Sassy said.
> "Tito told me you were ugly."

Myers's ear for dialogue remains unerring and, as in all his work, effectively delineates characters.

As has been seen in his other novels, Myers's view of the social agencies and institutions that are supposed to help the poor is not positive. His picture of the school Jamal attends is devastating. For reasons that are not apparent, Mr. Davidson, the principal, wants nothing more than to find an excuse to expel Jamal from the school. When the excuse comes in the form of the gun, which Jamal has taken to school to frighten the bully Dwayne, Mr. Davidson prefers to accept Jamal's denial rather than resolve the problem. The school authorities try medication to keep Jamal calm. Finally, Mr. Davidson uses an uncompleted homework assignment as the excuse to announce that Jamal will be transferred to a school for problem children. Only one teacher shows any sign of caring. It is a frightening vision.

The novel, a Newbery Honor book, is a powerful statement about the destructive potential of drugs and guns placed in the hands of poor and directionless young men along with promises of money and power. The book, however, is neither polemical nor sensational. The omniscient narrator keeps Jamal at the center, and Myers never violates that twelve-year-old's perspective. Because he makes us care about and believe in Jamal and Tito, and even though we sense from the moment Jamal accepts the gun there will be some kind of tragedy, we follow events hoping that tragedy will be averted.

In the end, the boys survive the battle, but it is uncertain whether they will survive the war. Tito is off to Puerto Rico, where we hope his emotional scars will heal. Jamal is left standing on the street, turning up his collar against the wind. His survival and healing remain questionable. There is no surrogate father waiting on the sidelines. His brother is fighting for his life in a prison hospital. School is no refuge. He has his family: a strong, sassy, but still young sister and a mother who loves her family and does her best but is herself nearly overwhelmed. As did Tippy and Crystal, he also has himself, stronger and wiser than before, having learned something about the poisonous sting of scorpions.

A Critical Look at the Urban Reality Novels

Over the decade in which these six novels appeared. Myers established himself with critics and reviewers as a skilled and gifted writer whose contributions to the field of adolescent literature are both noteworthy and significant. *School Library Journal* described *It Ain't All for Nothin'* as "a first-rate read."[3] Jeanne Betancourt refers to *Crystal* as "another fine book."[4] *Publisher's Weekly*, in its review of *Motown and Didi*, called Myers a "concerned and gifted writer."[5]

One of the strengths of these urban reality novels identified particularly, though not solely, by the *Bulletin of the Center for Children's Books* is Myers's ability to create believable, sympathetic characters. In its review of *It Ain't All for Nothin'*, the *Bulletin* notes that in spite of Tippy's undesirable behaviors, "He remains a sympathetic character, and in this first really serious book by Meyers [sic], that is one of the strengths: none of the characters is superficially drawn as all good or all bad. Not a happy book, but a trenchant and touching one."[6] The *Bulletin* also finds that in *Crystal*, "The milieu is convincingly detailed, the characterization and storyline equally believable."[7] Motown emerges for the *Bulletin* reviewer of *Motown and Didi* as "a common-man hero, a human being who has innate sweetness and delicacy along with all his strength."[8] *Horn Book* also finds that *Scorpions* has "well-developed characters."[9]

Not surprisingly, Myers has also won praise for his authentic rendering of the city environment that is the setting for these stories. *Booklist* notes in the review of *Hoops* the "sharply etched image of Harlem,"[10] and *School Library Journal* finds a "vivid slice of New York City life" in *It Ain't All for Nothin'*.[11]

Reviewers differ in their assessment of Myers's skill at constructing plots and his ability to develop a theme without becoming didactic. For example, *Booklist* finds that in *Crystal* "the plot is sometimes awkward, and the ultimate message is heavy."[12] On the other hand, Jeanne Betancourt thinks that *Crystal* is "a neatly constructed story,"[13] and *Publishers Weekly* finds it to be a "gripping story," though "something of a cautionary tale."[14]

The two basketball books also received contrasting assessments of their plots. *Booklist* found *Hoops* "somewhat uneven in the telling,"[15] and yet the same reviewer noted that *Outside Shot* "lacks the smooth, sure-footedness of the earlier book."[16] In contrast, the *Bulletin of the Center for Children's Books* found that in *Outside Shot* "sub-plots and themes are smoothly integrated."[17] Reviewers were generally in agreement, however, that Myers ably recreates the excitement of the action on and off the basketball court.

Myers brings to his characters a strong understanding of adolescence and a deep compassion and affection. *Booklist* notes that *It Ain't All for Nothin'* "retains the warmth and understanding, though not the humor, of *Fast Sam, Cool Clyde, and Stuff*."[18] The review of *Scorpions* in the *Bulletin of the Center for Children's Books* makes this point: "His compassion for Tito and Jamal is deep; perhaps the book's signal achievement is the way it makes us realize how young, in Harlem and elsewhere, twelve years old really is."[19]

As with the love and laughter novels, Myers's ability to create natural-sounding dialogue is recognized as another of his strengths. The *Horn Book* review of *Scorpions* says it best: "the dialogue is a finely tuned and paced vehicle for revealing character and issues."[20]

In these urban reality novels, Myers has combined memory and imagination to produce vivid portraits of ordinary people living in sometimes desperate circumstances. If there is an overarching theme, it is that survival, both psychological and physical, is possible even in those desperate circumstances. He celebrates the human spirit and the spirit and strength of a people whose survival has been achieved at great cost.

Because the books, with one exception, are set in a Black cultural milieu, they reflect some of the ways of living and believing that make Black culture distinct from other cultures in the United States. He has drawn on his knowledge of the Black church and its music to reveal aspects of character. Sprinkled throughout the novels are references to food, secular music, and names that are familiar to Blacks and that add to the authenticity of his setting. As in the love and laughter novels, Myers has played to his strength at reflecting the communication patterns typical of Black language use. When the situation seems to call for it, the language is strong, including some of the four-letter words that many librarians, teachers, and parents find offensive. Their use, however, is sparing and is actually milder than language used by many teenagers. Myers uses only enough such language to make his characters' speech seem authentic.

Unlike the love and laughter novels, in which the negative aspects of city living are a backdrop for the groups' humorous adventures, in these urban reality novels poverty, drugs, and violence often take center stage. The books are not, however, antidrug or antipoverty tracts. When poverty, violence, or drugs play a prominent role in these stories, it is because they play a prominent role in the everyday lives of ordinary Black people living in the Harlems of this country—not because they are drug users or perpetrators of violence, but because they have to protect themselves and their homes and families from those who are and who would corrupt their children.

It is significant that the young people in these novels, with the exception of Crystal, are fatherless, or virtually so. Tippy's father is weak and ineffectual; Motown's is likely dead. The fathers of Didi, Lonnie, and Jamal have abandoned their families because they were unable or unwilling to provide for them. This is in stark contrast to the love and laughter novels, in which fathers played a central role in the lives of their sons. The women who care for the protagonists are a mixed lot. Grandma Carrie becomes ill; Didi's mother needs mothering herself. Lonnie's and Jamal's mothers are doing their best, fighting their battles virtually alone. The odds against the survival of the young people in these novels are made worse by the absence of a strong, two-parent family.

Part of the power of Myers's work is that it reveals how the lack of money renders people powerless and often places them at the mercy of agencies and institutions and the strangers who run them. One of the most poignant scenes in these six novels is the one in which Grandma Carrie in *It Ain't All for Nothin'* confronts the welfare workers and the police in her effort to get help. A canny neighbor has figured out a way to get the social agencies to come to her. She has called the police and reported that Tippy was being abused. Two welfare workers and a policeman investigate and inform Grandma Carrie that she must go to the welfare office to apply. She has no money for a taxi and is unable to walk to the subway. "I got to lay up here and die before you takes notice that I need something? . . . I've been a working woman all my life—I ain't asking for nothing 'cause I don't want to work. She started crying, and it was the first time I had seen her cry like that. She was crying deep from her chest, and tears was running down her face."

Myers also shows how lack of money and the lack of prospects for legitimate ways to obtain it can motivate people to make wrong choices. He reveals, too, how poverty does not prevent poor Black people from sharing the dreams, ambitions, and values of the larger society—a full refrigerator, a loving family, a peaceful drug-free neighborhood, college, a good marriage, a lucrative career, the good life.

In these six novels Myers succeeds in doing what all fine literature does: he illuminates the human condition, offering insights into life and living. Myers books are compelling enough and engaging enough that his readers will have lived with the characters, if briefly, in a difficult time and place. The books offer those readers both insight into what it is like to struggle under such circumstances and a strong sense of hope because they have seen that survival is possible. They are a singular achievement.

4. Of Mystery and Adventure: Myers the Storyteller

Afro-American novelist may be the most important role Myers plays as a writer, but it is not the only one. Not all his books focus on vertical living in New York City, nor are all his protagonists Black. He enjoys writing in various genres about various topics. Further, the market for books about Blacks is perceived by the publishing industry to be small; only a few are published each year. Thus, most Black authors of juvenile books hold other jobs to supplement their incomes. (Myers and Virginia Hamilton are the two exceptions that come to mind.) In Myers's case, he sometimes turns to writing lighter pieces that he can do quickly and easily, some of which he himself refers to as "fluff."

Although this lighter material may not put Myers on the road to a Newbery medal, it need not be dismissed as unworthy. Myers knows how to create credible characters and an easygoing first-person narration. He also knows how to write humor, create suspense, and keep a plot moving: he is a good storyteller. In these books, Myers uses all these talents and offers foreign settings, intrigue, mystery, and adventure.

The Arrow Adventures

The fluff includes the Arrow Adventure Series, published by Viking Puffin. To date there have been four Arrow Adventures: *Adventure in Granada, The Hidden Shrine, Duel in the Desert*, and *Ambush in the Amazon*. They feature the escapades of Chris and Ken Arrow, white teenagers, who travel with their anthropologist mother, Carla, as she studies family life in various parts of the world: Peru, Hong Kong, Spain, and Morocco. Their father, a mythologist, disappeared years ago on an archeological expedition in Mexico, and now the boys are seventeen and fourteen.

Inevitably, Carla Arrow's work takes her away from her sons so that the boys are left on their own. A local teenager, somehow connected to one of Carla Arrow's colleagues, becomes guide, translator, and accomplice for the boys. The adventure involves some local problem: a stolen object, unexplained events. Villains shoot at them, kidnap them, try various means to frighten them away from their investigations, but the clever boys and their companion always manage to outsmart or outrun them. In the end, right prevails, and the villains are turned over to local authorities.

The books are between eighty-three and ninety pages long; the plots are fast moving and allow little room (and little need, given the intent to entertain) for character development. The Arrow brothers, however, do have distinct personalities. Ken, the younger, is very bright and loves to play with language. One of his puns usually ends each book, accompanied by groans all around. Part of the fun of the books is to watch for the clever puns he uses in conversations with his mother when he wants to avoid telling her the whole truth about their current adventures. When Chris has his nose bloodied by a villain who butted him with his head, Ken's telephone report to his mother on the day's activities includes comments about having spent the day nosing around and finding out that the people of Hong Kong aren't just running around; they know how to use their heads as well.

Chris, the inquisitive and determined first-person narrator, plays the older brother role by teasing and verbally sparring with Ken, reminding him of his place as the younger sibling. But there is affection between the two boys; their sparring never lasts long enough to interfere with the action and never gets nasty enough to keep the boys apart for long. Chris also acknowledges Ken's clever ideas, which usually help solve the mystery at hand. When Ken is in trouble, nothing will stop Chris from trying to rescue him.

As usual, the dialogue sounds natural, and in keeping with the focus on adventure, it is also brisk. The first-person narration provides a "you-are-there" feeling. Action dominates, and the exotic settings add to the sense of adventure and provide just a glimpse of life in far-off places—tourist sites, local foods, markets, and animals.

Tales of a Dead King

Egypt is the setting for *Tales of a Dead King*, another brief mystery adventure. The white teenagers this time are Karen Lacey, and John Robie, the narrator. They have gone to Egypt to assist John's great-uncle, the famous archeologist Dr. Erich Leonhardt (an Eric Leonhardt was Myers's best friend in childhood), on a dig. When the teenagers arrive in Aswan, however, Dr. Leonhardt has mysteriously disappeared. John and Karen decide to stay around for a few days, and strange things start happening: a snake is found in Karen's bed; a stranger in a green hat follows them; someone throws a dagger in their direction. They piece together some clues and decide that Dr. Leonhardt might have met with foul play. Following up on the clues, they discover that he has been kidnapped by greedy local citizens who are after the treasure they believe to be in the tomb he was seeking. Predictably, all ends well, and John and Karen get a chance to do some real archeological work.

Myers's sense of humor is apparent again in puns and in the narration. Karen is often just a step ahead of John in her thinking, and he finds this rather annoying, though he handles it with a bit of self-deprecating good humor. He may be outclassed—but then again, not necessarily. There is enough tension between John and Karen to keep things interesting and to suggest the possibility of a future romance. The narration is easygoing; the pace is brisk; the characters are believable, even if their escapades are a bit far-fetched. The Egyptian setting and the archeological focus permits Myers to include some reference to Egyptian history and mythology, but for the most part such information serves the story by providing clues or contexts for understanding possible motivations.

Adventure in a Serious Vein

Two of Myers's adventure books, *The Nicholas Factor* and *The Legend of Tarik*, are more serious and do not belong in the fluff category. In the tradition of the romantic adventure story, each features a hero who takes a perilous journey and triumphs over evil forces. Gerald, the hero of *The Nicholas Factor*, is a contemporary young man whose only weapon is his brain but who has access to the modern magic of airplanes, money, and fast cars. Tarik is an ancient knight who fights with a magic sword and rides a wonder horse. Both, however, raise some of the same questions about how to determine right from wrong. At the decisive moment, both choose to do what has to be done, and both return from their journeys having taken major steps toward manhood.

Intrigue in the Amazon: *The Nicholas Factor*

Publishers Weekly calls *The Nicholas Factor* "a disturbing, powerful work."[1] It is a suspenseful book in which Myers takes the exotic setting and the mystery and intrigue of the adventure series and adds a touch of romance. He also dips back into the love and laughter novels for the idea of a good-doing group of young people. This time, however, he brushes the group with a streak of evil.

The good-doing group is the Crusade Society, an elitist international organization of the best and the brightest teenagers, committed to getting involved in the world they will someday lead. The founder, Marlin Wilkes, was inspired by the story of Nicholas, a young leader of the Children's Crusade. The Nicholas Factor is the potential power of a committed group of bright young men and women to change the world. In Marlin's view such a group could help make a positive difference in the world. In the view of the villain such a group could rule the world.

Gerald McQuillen, a college student, is asked by a government security agent to join the Crusaders and to report any suspicious or unusual happenings he observes. He accepts the assignment even though he thinks it's a snobbish group, and goes off with the group to Peru to participate in an experiment designed to get the Quechua Indians to wear shoes to protect them from a local parasite. It soon becomes clear that the project is a cover for a sinister plot by a right-wing German Crusader who plans to take over the group. Things start to go terribly wrong. Gerald's roommate, Andwele, is poisoned, Indians start dying, and the project is abruptly called off. Gerald escapes the jungle with his friend Jennifer and the fatally ill Andwele, but he is pursued by the villains, who know he has evidence of their wrongdoing. With help from the government agent they successfully elude the pursuers, and Gerald returns home older and wiser.

Within its realism, the novel incorporates many elements of the traditional romantic adventure. The structure is circular. Gerald McQuillen sets off on a perilous journey: if Kohler, the German villain, suspects that Gerald is involved with the agency, his life will be in danger. Further, if the Crusaders learn of his involvement, he is likely to be ostracized by his peers, since many college students mistrust CIA-like organizations. Gerald suffers through an ordeal, a test of his courage and wits. Once Kohler realizes that Gerald and Jennifer know about the deaths of the Indians and are escaping with evidence, he uses every means at his disposal, including physical assault and shooting, to stop them. Gerald loses a friend: Andwele dies before they can get him to a hospital. Ultimately, Gerald is successful, however; he hands the evidence over to the agent, learns that Kohler has been arrested, and returns safely home, where his mother waits.

As with any good adventure story, the plot is a strong element of the book. The suspense begins in the first chapter with the unusual call from the dean of Gerald's college asking him to meet—off campus—with someone who is interested in the work of the college. There is enough mystery and stealth about John Martens and the way he works to keep curiosity aroused during the preparation period before the trip. Myers keeps Gerald in California just long enough to get him into the group, bring him to the attention of Marlin, and get him invited to Peru. Once they arrive in Peru, suspense builds, and events move quickly to the exciting climax. Since Gerald narrates the story, there are still loose ends dangling after his escape—information about events and motivations previously unknown to Gerald. Myers ties these loose ends together in a final chapter, set at the airport in California, in which John provides Gerald with all the information he needs to understand what had happened.

Reviewers disagreed not only on the strength of the plot but on the credibility of the characters. The *Bulletin of the Center for Children's Books* found the story "artfully structured, with good pace and suspense, and . . . developed with both logic and drama."[2] *School Library Journal*, on the other hand, stated that "The book does not deliver the tension and sense of danger it tells us about, and too many arcane motives must be explained in the last chapter. But because the characters are realistically presented, . . . this should be an appealing, popular adventure."[3]

Where SLJ found realistic characters, *Kirkus* found that "the implausible motivation of all the Crusaders, villains and dupes alike, requires an overgenerous suspension of belief."[4] *Hornbook*, too, had difficulty with the characterization but approved the plotting: "Although the characterizations are thin and unsupported, the plot is full of twists, and the dangers of an elitist society are made clear."[5]

Any shortcomings in the plot may have to do with credibility and may arise partly from the genre. Adventure stories tend to exaggerate the adventures and abilities of the hero. Gerald's bribing his way to Lima is fairly sophisticated for a seventeen-year-old, and the car chase scene is low-key Hollywood. But this is a world peopled with CIA-like agents and an international organization of idealistic, superintelligent teenagers, and given those premises the plot is not as far-fetched as it might be.

Characters in romantic adventures are typically not very well developed and often are representatives of types. Some of the characters in *The Nicholas Factor* function as types. Kohler is the cold, completely evil villain. Like Touchy in *Motown and Didi*, he was abused as a child and does not like to be touched. He keeps a bodyguard as a shield between him and warm human beings. Alfredo, with his open collars, gold chains, and good looks, is the overconfident, swaggering foil for Gerald's watchful skepticism.

John Martens, the Black federal agent, provides some of the wisdom and help that the traditional hero often receives from an older mentor or kind spirit. Gerald refers to him as a "guardian angel." He gives Gerald a supply of Peruvian money, stands by in Lima while Gerald is off in the jungle with the Crusaders, and has a car waiting when Gerald and Jennifer desperately need one to escape. Before Gerald leaves for Peru, he and John have discussions about right and wrong, about truth, and about the necessity to continually examine one's beliefs.

As a security agent, Martens is not forthcoming with much personal information about himself—another reason he is not a developed character. He does, however, provide some humor. In one case, he is the vehicle for Myers's sly dig at the "all Blacks look alike" shibboleth. When Martens visits the drug store where Gerald works, a coworker wants to know if he is Richard Pryor. John has a sense of humor similar to Myers's own. He relates a silly story about alcoholic bedbugs and at one point suggests skunk juice as a remedy for mosquito bites: if you spread it all over yourself, you'll forget about mosquito bites.

The three Crusaders who are best delineated are Jennifer, the romantic interest; Andwele, Gerald's African roommate; and, of course, Gerald. Jennifer is a distinct individual, if not one who is easy for ordinary teenagers to identify with. She is very bright and wealthy but another of Myers's vulnerable young women with a tough outer shell. Myers gives us enough details about her troubled relationship with her father to offer insight into both her toughness and her vulnerability.

There are fewer details about Andwele. He is from the Cameroon, the son of a finance minister, and has been told by his uncle that he has the "spirit of a turtle." Andwele is a questioner who offers to his two American friends a third world perspective on projects such as the one they are working on in Peru. Having experienced the effects of colonialism, Andwele shares valuable insights.

Gerald, the hero, is a developed character. As a result of his experiences in the jungle, he loses some of his innocence and grows from uncertainty to a clearer sense of who he is. He even reaches his symbolic eighteenth birthday the day before the project falls apart. On one level, Gerald's is a simple quest for information. He wants to know if the Crusaders have been infiltrated by a right-wing extremist group. On another level, as is usual with romances, he is on a quest for self-discovery. He is intrigued by the potential danger involved in investigating the Crusade Society and likes the idea of possibly becoming a hero.

Unlike the traditional romantic hero, however, Gerald has concerns both about the validity of his quest and whether he is capable of achieving it. The anticipation of becoming a hero is clouded by the memory of a moment when, driving a racing car, imagining himself taking his father's place, he had been nearly overcome with fear. "When the time came, I had thought, I wouldn't be up to it." When he is faced with a crisis in the Amazon jungle, however, he discovers that he has the courage and the will to do what he thinks is right. But his sense of victory is not complete. It is diminished by Andwele's death and by the death and suffering of the Peruvians.

If Gerald was seeking knowledge about himself and what kind of man he would be "when the time came," Myers was also raising questions of a more general nature. In one passage, he returns to an important theme from the urban novels: the importance of community, the need to belong and be linked with others like yourself. Gerald observed the anguish of the Peruvian guide,

Tasso, when he saw his people sick and dying and recognized that in the moment of his anguish Tasso had rediscovered a strong connection to his own people. Gerald wonders whether the Crusaders—in fact, all crusaders—were not simply seeking that kind of connection, needing "to touch each other, to know they were not alone in a hostile world."

In *The Nicholas Factor* Myers postulates an elitist group set up to do good in the world. Then he asks us to consider what might go wrong with such a group if individual members stop examining their beliefs and if their own status as the best and the brightest becomes more important than the good they set out to do. Myers does not give easy answers but suggests that idealism on an individual level works—that "our greatest danger is that right-minded people will be apathetic."

Adventure in North Africa: *The Legend of Tarik*

The Legend of Tarik is Myers's venture into the fantasy novel, where Black heroes, indeed Black characters of any kind, are rare. The hero in this case is a young Black knight from West Africa seeking revenge for the murder of his people. Tariq (Tarik) ibn Ziyad is the name of the Moorish governor of Tangier, a Muslim who, in the eighth century, defeated Roderic, the last Visigoth King of Spain, and gave his name to the Rock of Gibraltar. Gibraltar is a corruption of "Jabal Tariq" (Mount Tarik). Myers could find very little information in English about Tarik, so he created his own legend.

In keeping with the mythlike quality of the story, Myers has abandoned his easygoing narrative style for one more formal and solemn. Like the Christmas story in the gospel of Luke, it begins "It came to pass," and like the rest of the New Testament, it is sprinkled with parables and aphorisms. A biblical influence can also be seen in the structure of sentences and in the choice of figurative language: "Ntah, a man of stubborn pride, tried to lift himself above the war, even as an eagle lifts itself above the tops of mountains to catch the stirring winds." *Booklist* found the style "stately."[6] On the other hand, Ethel Twitchell, writing for *Horn Book*, found it "stilted, self conscious," and sometimes "weighty."[7] The language is a clear signal that Myers's intent was to create something beyond a simple adventure story.

The book is divided into two parts. The first part describes in detail Tarik's training and preparation for the quest he must complete. When the aptly named El Muerte invades the land where Tarik and his family settled, he captures Tarik, his father, and his brother and takes them away. Tarik sees his father and brother slaughtered for sport by El Muerte and his men. Left for dead, Tarik is rescued by Docao, an old white priest whose own family was killed and whose hand was severed by El Muerte. Docao and Nongo, an elderly Black teacher from West Africa who was blinded by El Muerte, become Tarik's trainers and mentors.

Once Tarik learns to control his anger and to sense the life force in people and objects, his training begins. He and Stria, a young woman who also was taken in by Docao and Nongo, are trained as warriors. Before he goes to fight, Tarik must acquire three things: a magic sword, a crystal of truth, and a magnificent and magical black horse named Zinzinbadio. To obtain them he must use his intellect as well as his physical strength. He has to fight two horrifying monsters and get close enough to the horse to claim him as his own.

The second part describes his adventures and final triumph over El Muerte. Stria has followed him on his journey, and they are later joined by a baker who provides some comic relief from the grisly encounters with El Muerte's advance guard. When El Muerte has finally been dispatched, Stria rides away alone, Capa the baker returns to his fat wife, and Tarik turns his horse south toward the Niger River and home.

True to the tradition of the heroic myth, most of the characters are not three-dimensional: they are types or symbols: his teachers are wise, the baker is loyal, El Muerte is evil incarnate. Stria is obsessed with the need for vengeance and is symbolic of the madness of single-minded, uncontrolled rage. She is also an intriguing character, however. Docao describes her as "like a guitar that one strums seeking the soothing sounds of a sweet tune but that responds only with the most violent discord." She too saw her people slaughtered by El Muerte and became nearly consumed with hatred for him. On one hand, Stria's obsession for revenge concentrates her strength so that she is a formidable fighter. Her training sessions with Tarik strike another blow for feminism and help him change some of his culturally conditioned male chauvinist views on the roles of females. At first Tarik wonders why she is not serving the men: "It is the use of a bowl to hold water." One session of fighting Stria lets him know that she is no serving vessel; she would have fought to the death had she not been stopped. Stria stubbornly follows Tarik on his journey, wearing her coat of mail, fighting fiercely when necessary, saving his life on occasion. She wants only to see El Muerte dead. On the other hand, she is not so mad or empty that she cannot nurse Tarik's wounds or recognize the good in Docao, Nongo, and Tarik, and regret that, even after El Muerte is killed, she still feels empty; she has no kind words to give Tarik. "They have all been taken from me."

Tarik is, in most ways, the archetypal hero. He experiences a symbolic death and then a rebirth in the gardens of Shange. During his training period he must pass three tests and thereby gain wisdom. In addition to wisdom, Tarik acquires, with the help of his mentors, magic objects to help him accomplish his ultimate task. Before he is sent on his mission, Nongo laments that they cannot perform the initiation rites that would have marked Tarik's passage into manhood in his society. There is "no shadow of pain . . . , no charm . . . , no forbidden lodge." Nevertheless, Tarik is expected to "close his eyes as a child, and open them into manhood," a symbolic initiation. His quest is clear; he must kill El Muerte and revenge the slaughter of his people. It is the classic clash between good and evil, and Tarik, who is told by Stria that he is Good (with a capital *G*), triumphs.

Unlike the traditional hero, however, Tarik comes to question the rightness of his quest. During his training, he is generally cocky, and after he has obtained the sword, the crystal, and the horse, he thinks he is ready to fulfill a hundred quests. He has moments of doubt, however. He remembers an incident when, as a child, he bragged to his mother that he would be a warrior and kill all the warriors in the village in order to become king. His mother made him kill a chicken for his supper. The task was most unpleasant, and when he went to her crying, she pushed him away, telling him that once he learned to kill, he could no longer be a child. Remembering, Tarik, like Gerald, wonders whether when the time comes, he will be able to kill El Muerte.

Before the ultimate battle with El Muerte, he has a number of violent and gruesome encounters, during which he kills several men. He grows weary of the killing and realizes that his mother was right; he will never again be the child she knew. The killing begins to seem too easy, and he recognizes that the choice between right and wrong, good and evil, is not always clear. He questions whether the real gift that Docao and Nongo have given him is only the gift to kill easily. Stria insists that it is the gift to do what must be done. He recognizes that when the time comes he will use that gift and make that choice. Violence must sometimes be answered with violence.

The plentiful violence in *Tarik* no doubt contributed to its mixed reviews. Hazel Rochman found it "a powerful tale," that "makes clear that the heroic quest is also an arduous search for self-knowledge and identity."[8] In stark contrast is the scathing review from the *Voice of Youth Advocates*, which does not recognize the book as a heroic adventure and finds it to be "an awful book. There is so much predictability in the shallow characters and situations that the mean-spirited violence is almost welcome, but not quite. . . . This book neither edifies nor satisfies."[9]

Most reviews, however, are mixed, and where one reviewer sees strength, another sees weakness. Where *Booklist* finds "vivid detail without slowing down the pace,"[10] Malcolm Bosse finds "a thinness of detail, particularly in descriptions of the physical setting."[11] But Bosse also thought *Tarik* to be "an admirably paced novel with plenty of action,"[12] contrasting with Ethel Twichell's assessment, which is representative of the reviews that recognized both the strengths and weaknesses of the novel. "The pace is uneven with a slow, deliberate beginning and a greatly accelerated denouement. Yet the flaws notwithstanding, there are moments of excitement and tension, and the author has a talent for creating repulsive monsters. The elements of a good story are here; one wishes it could have been fleshed out in a more convincing way."[13]

It is tempting to read *The Legend of Tarik* as an allegorical statement about a people freeing themselves from oppression. Tarik is, after all, a Black African knight who, in the name of his people, rids the world of an evil white oppressor. Today's readers live in a society where racism is rampant, and whether or not Myers intended to make such a statement, he does offer some wisdom for young readers, particularly those who see themselves as members of an oppressed group, to ponder. He warns them of the dangers of letting anger control their lives and of becoming blinded by hate. Although the evil one is white, those fighting on the side of good are black and white and tan, as are those who have suffered. Before the hero is ready to fight, he is required to learn three important lessons. The first is that though evil can take many forms, he has to face it squarely and see it for what it is. The second is that he must be willing to confront truth, regardless of the risks. Finally, he has to learn that his mind can be as potent a weapon as a sword. These are ideas any reader would do well to ponder.

5. Of Battles and Brotherhood: Myers the War Novelist

Lord let us feel pity for Private Jenkins, and sorrow for ourselves, and all the angel warriors that fall. Let us fear death, but let it not live within us. Protect us, O Lord, and be merciful unto us. Amen.

This is the prayer that gives *Fallen Angels* its title, offered on the death of one of the angel warriors—boys sent off to fight wars before they are old enough to vote. A disproportionate percentage of those angel warriors were underprivileged young men who could not escape the draft or who thought the military would offer them educational opportunities and a source of income. Many were from the Harlems of this country, and in *Fallen Angels* Myers presents a fictional portrayal of one such young man and his experience of the Vietnam War.

The book is dedicated to Myers's brother Tommy, one of the several Martinsburg siblings who made their way to New York. Although Myers did not develop close relationships with them, the younger boys admired Walter, who had escaped the hardships of Martinsburg and lived what must have appeared to be an exciting life in Harlem. Tommy, a sensitive young man who wanted to be an artist, elected first to follow his older brother's footsteps and join the army. He became one of the fallen angels, struck down before his twenty-first birthday. Myers was deeply moved by his death and terribly saddened at the thought of the wasted life—a gift thrown away.

Even though the book honors Tommy, Myers tapped his own experiences to create the character of Richard Perry. Like Myers, he attended Stuyvesant High School and wanted to go to college and become a writer. They both joined the army at seventeen, were stationed at Fort Devens, and played basketball for the army. In his speeches and in his autobiographical writings, Myers often acknowledges a debt to his high school English teacher, Bonnie Liebow, for the individualized reading list she gave him. In a tribute to his teacher, Myers names Perry's English teacher Mrs. Liebow and the fictional Mrs. Liebow makes a comment about heroism that states one of the themes of the book. Perry tells her about a feeling he sometimes has: "I would feel a pressure to give in, to let a rebound go over my head, to take the outside shot when I knew I had to take the ball inside. . . . I told Mrs. Liebow, my English teacher, and she had said that it was what separated heroes from humans, the not giving in, and I hadn't understood that."

But Perry is not, after all, Myers; *Fallen Angels* is not autobiography. Myers did not fight in Vietnam, and *Fallen Angels* is a testament to his craft as a creator of realistic fiction. The book is a graphic and sometimes horrifying depiction of the waste, the futility, and the anguish of war. It is also, as Mel Watkins points out in the *New York Times Book Review*, "as much about Perry's coming of age as it is about the Vietnam War."[1]

Fallen Angels shares with *The Nicholas Factor* and *The Legend of Tarik* the structure of the romantic adventure story. Richard Perry, too, takes a circular journey. The book begins with Perry on his way to Vietnam and closes with him on his way home. There the similarity to a romance ends. What he does share with Gerald and Tarik is a loss of innocence, the passage to manhood, and the realization that, in the real world, issues of right and wrong, good and evil, are not easily decided.

Fallen Angels opens with Richard Perry on his way to Vietnam in 1967. He chooses to join the army rather than enroll in City College because he thinks his military pay will help his mother and younger brother. He plays basketball for an army team, injures his knee, and is supposed to be excused from combat duty. But through an army snafu, he is sent to Vietnam. Much of his time there is spent waiting, bored, hoping that rumors of imminent peace are true. Other time is spent on patrol, on "pacification missions," in combat. People who share those kinds of experiences develop a bond, and camaraderie grows among the members of Perry's squad. The book ends with Perry on his way back to "the World" some months later, wounded but essentially whole, presumably with a clearer understanding of Mrs. Liebow's definition of heroism.

The Craft of *Fallen Angels*

Reviewers recognized *Fallen Angels* as an extraordinary book. *School Library Journal*, in a starred review, called it "a riveting account of the Vietnam War" and "a compelling, graphic, necessarily gruesome, and wholly plausible novel. It neither condemns nor glorifies the war but certainly causes readers to think about events."[2] *Horn Book* also gave it a starred review, in which Ethel Heins found that "Except for occasional outbursts, the narration is remarkably direct and understated; and the dialogue, with morbid humor sometimes adding comic relief, is steeped in natural vulgarity, without which verisimilitude would be unthinkable. . . . With its intensity and vividness in depicting a young soldier amid the chaos and the carnage of war, the novel recalls Stephen Crane's *The Red Badge of Courage*."[3]

In this book Myers brings together all those elements of his craft that make his best writing commendable. His characters are complex and memorable. The dialogue, both in Black vernacular and standard informal English, sounds genuine and is a major means by which he defines his characters. He uses imagery and figurative language to paint vivid word pictures of the setting, the action, and the characters. There is both linguistic and situational humor. His first-person narrator keeps the reader close to the action, and he skillfully draws the reader into sharing the emotions of his characters. The descriptions of the fighting are dramatic.

Richard Perry is drawn as an ordinary young man from Harlem—bright, fatherless, without enough money to ensure a smooth passage even through City College. He tells us that in high school he had so few suitable clothes that he had to wash them every night and dry them each morning on the oven door. Clothes for college seemed like an impossibility. Besides his mother, who drinks too much, he leaves at home a younger brother, Kenny, for whom he feels responsible. For Perry, as for many poor young men, the army seems to offer a reasonable alternative to the streets or to the college education that was out of his reach—some training, a temporary job, a salary for his family.

Mrs. Liebow points out that Perry is "too young to be just an observer in life." Readers need Perry to be an observer, however, since through him we come to know the other soldiers and to experience all the action. Partly because he is an observer, he has developed a sensitivity, an ability to tune in to the feelings of those around him. He understands when it is appropriate to reach out to his cohorts and when to keep quiet and leave them with their thoughts. He knows intuitively how to compose a letter to the family of a fallen comrade that is touching and eloquent in its simplicity.

Perry is more than an observer, however. Although he is no "gung ho" soldier, he is prepared to do his part once he has been assigned to a squad. Given the opportunity to opt out of patrols because of his knee, he elects to participate with the others. That decision sets the stage for him to experience the full horror of the war. He learns to live with "the fear that calls each of our names." He sees people dying all around him and even confronts his own death when a Vietcong guerilla tries to shoot him in the head, failing only because his gun malfunctions. Perry shoots the attacker's face away and is shaken both by his close call with death and by his killing another human being not by shooting at some bushes but at close range.

If this is a coming-of-age story, then as Mel Watkins points out, "Perry's experience in Vietnam—his baptism in the violence, confusion and moral havoc—is the crucible that tests and determines his passage to manhood."[4] Having arrived in Vietnam an innocent, he leaves understanding that war changes humans, that it sometimes even destroys their humanity. He also knows that he has survived because, like Mrs. Liebow's heroes, he hasn't given in.

The character who becomes Perry's best buddy, and who provides most of the much needed humor in *Fallen Angels* is Peewee Gates, high school dropout from Chicago. Peewee is almost always talking—teasing, challenging, spouting opinions and his philosophy of life. The first line of the book is his:

> "Somebody must have told them suckers I was coming."
> "Told who?" I [Perry] asked.
> "The Congs, man. Who you think I'm talking 'bout?"
> "Why you think somebody told them you were coming?
> "Cause I don't see none of 'em around here. They don't want their butts kicked."

No matter that the troops are in Anchorage, Alaska, on a refueling stop. Peewee is on his way, and he is *bad*!

Peewee is another young man from a poor inner-city neighborhood. He has joined the army, he says, because when he accompanied a friend to the recruiting office, the friend, who had a criminal record, was rejected because the army does not take rowdies. He figured that if the army were serious about killing people, they would most certainly look first for "them suckers from the projects, 'cause that's all they like to do, anyway." He now thinks he's been tricked. The army is deadly serious.

Peewee takes on all comers, regardless of size or position. His armor against fear and danger is to take the offensive, to openly invite them into his territory. When a white soldier, much larger than he, calls him "boy," Peewee kicks him in the groin and threatens him with a switchblade. When Johnson, a large Black soldier, tired of hearing Peewee belittle his native Georgia, declares that Chicago is nothing, Peewee's retort—"Neither is your daddy"— signals that Peewee is unimpressed by Johnson's size. When a captain asks, "Where the hell is your pride, soldier?" Peewee's reply is "In Chicago, sir. Can I go get it?" Perry speculates that Peewee likes to court danger.

Peewee, however, is not simply a clown, inserted into the novel to provide comic relief. Beneath the protective shell of his rhetoric, Peewee is the boy who wants to mingle spit with Perry in order to seal a vow of brotherhood and who smears a homemade Vietnamese salve on his upper lip in order to grow a mustache. His three ambitions are to drink wine from a bottle with a cork, smoke a cigar, and make love with a foreign woman. He is also a young man deeply hurt by his girlfriend's "Dear John" letter and deeply shaken by witnessing the death of a soldier holding a booby-trapped Vietnamese child for whom Peewee was busy making a doll. He is most of all, however, Perry's friend, sitting with him through a bad case of diarrhea, holding him when he can't shake the horror of having nearly been killed, helping him to recognize that, for the common soldier, the war was simply about killing or being killed. When Peewee finally acknowledges the possibility that he might actually die in combat, he verbally wills to Perry the only material thing of value he owns, an old coin.

Others in the squad are well-defined individuals, too. Notable among them are Johnson, the veteran about whom there is "a knowing" that could be trusted in or out of battle; Monaco, the Italian who is friendly enough with the Blacks to be considered one of them; and Lobel, the Jew who casts his lot with the Blacks and who copes with the war by making it all into a mental movie—until he kills his first enemy soldier, "up close, . . . personal," and it becomes real. In the beginning there were five whites and five Blacks from varying backgrounds. The eight who survive forge a bond cemented by their dependence on each other for survival in the "deep boonies" of Vietnam.

Richard Perry is older than all Myers's first-person narrators except Lonnie Jackson, the basketball player in *Hoops*. Partly because he is older, Perry's is a more literary voice, using strong imagery to paint vivid word pictures, particularly when the troops are on patrol or in firefights:

> It was grave dark and quiet except for the things that crawled in the night.
>
> There were shadows all around me, laughing, jerking, mocking.
>
> The chopper came and we handed up Lieutenant Carroll. A burnt offering.
>
> [on helicopters]: Great insects, angry and buzzing over the steaming jungle.
>
> The chopper crews. They were the stuff of heroes. Swooping from the skies like great heavenly birds gathering the angels who had fallen below.

Lobel's repeated references to filmmaking and the possible roles the soldiers are playing become a part of an extended metaphor in which Myers contrasts the reality of war with the romantic notions perpetrated by movies and television. Lobel's uncle is a film director, so he is familiar with the illusions that Hollywood creates. Early on he suggests that the way to end the war is to take all the Vietcong to Universal Studios and give them bit parts in war movies. On guard duty, he declares that he cannot decide what part he is playing: the star in the foxhole who survives, Lee Marvin as a tough sergeant, or the baby-faced virgin who gets shot. His advice to Perry is to stay away from the role of "the good black guy who everybody thinks is a coward and then gets killed trying to save everybody else."

Perry, too, is a movie lover whose all-time favorite film is *Shane*. He can easily join in conversations with Lobel. He struggles with letters to his brother so that Kenny will not get the idea that war is like the movies. In a battle scene, Perry desperately wishes it were: "I didn't want to get up. Where the hell was the popcorn machine?"

When the men are sitting around the barracks, the pace of the book slows considerably. Very little happens, and these sections depict for the reader how the boredom, the waiting, and the lack of anything productive to do can lead to bickering and exacerbate the tensions that arise when people of various backgrounds, facing serious danger, spend time together in confined spaces. The menu is repeated so often—roast beef, mashed potatoes, peas, carrots, carrot cake, and milk—that once the cooks have to serve it wearing flak jackets. By repeating the entire menu each time it is served. Myers gives the reader a sense of the monotony experienced by the soldiers who had to eat it. A Julie Andrews movie is viewed three times—the last time without the sound and with the soldiers playing the parts. A broken television set, vicious mosquitoes, insect repellent so strong it keeps Perry awake—the details relate the sense of ennui. One of Perry's discoveries is that on some level the war is about "hours of boredom, seconds of terror."

In contrast to the boredom of the barracks, the fight scenes—the seconds of terror—are dramatic and gruesome. Myers uses stomach-tightening descriptions of the horrors of battle to undercut any sense of war as romantic adventure. We are forced to witness the sickening and grisly details of the deaths of men and boys on both sides of the war, as well as Vietnamese civilians. This violence is controlled and grows out of the setting, but there is enough to hammer home the point that war is hell and that it sometimes encourages people to forget, at least temporarily, their humanity.

Images of body bags appear more than once. When the first member of the squad is killed by a mine, Perry is sent to get the body bag. The large supply of bags on the shelf reminds Perry that many soldiers were expected to die in this place. When another squad member dies next to him in a helicopter where they both lie wounded, the use of the body bag confirms the death for Perry: "I heard the zipper. I didn't have to see it. I heard the zipper." The understatement is as effective as a graphic description of a mutilated and torn body. There is no shortage of such graphic descriptions, however: "I could see bubbles of blood coming from a gaping wound in his throat. The flies around the pile, crawling over the bodies, into and out of the wound, buzzed in delight."

Most of the time, however, Perry's narrative voice is like those of most of Myers's first-person narrators—direct, conversational. The point of view is consistently Perry's, and Myers makes effective use of Perry's memories and recollections to fill in information about his background and to round out his characterization. We learn of his conflicts with his mother: he was bright, and she never understood his needs. We also learn how much he loves his younger brother Kenny and how he takes seriously his role of older brother and role model.

Most of what we learn about the other characters comes from their conversation and from Perry's observations about them. Perry reports the dialogue that goes on among the men in the barracks and in the field. Again, Myers's rendition of the Black vernacular of Peewee and the other Black soldiers reflects his clear understanding of its grammar and style, although Peewee, unlike some of the younger boys in the love and laughter novels, is no young adolescent showing off his rapping ability. Myers is equally adept at creating natural-sounding speech for his white characters.

The dialogue also reflects the kind of language that is likely to be heard among men in wartime, words that many consider profane or foul. There is a generous sprinkling of such language throughout the book but not to the extent to which it is used in reality. Myers uses enough to give the flavor of barracks talk. His retort to people who consider the language obscene is to remind them that the real obscenity was the war itself.

The Vietnam War raised many issues that were debated in the streets and in the homes of America. *Fallen Angels* touches on several: the practice of promoting officers on the basis of the numbers of enemy killed, leading to the falsifying of body counts: the racism that caused some officers to give the most dangerous assignments to Blacks and that encouraged Americans to refer to the Vietnamese as "gooks"; the massacre of Vietnamese civilians; the mix-ups in which Americans fought and killed other Americans. He also raises questions about the effects of the war on the Vietnamese civilian population. Myers, however, is not on a soapbox. These issues are embedded in the context of the war experiences of Perry and his cohorts and are presented as events to which the soldiers respond in various ways.

The major issue, however, and the one Perry wrestles with repeatedly is "Why are we here?" When, near the beginning of the novel, a television news crew asks the squad members why they are fighting in Vietnam, all except Peewee give idealistic answers about fighting communism, believing in the domino theory, and demonstrating that America stands for something. Perry's answer is that "we either defended our country abroad, or we would be forced to fight in the streets of America." As the war goes on, however, his certainty evaporates. He recognizes that the war may seem right from a distance but when the killing begins there is no right or wrong, only endurance and survival; that in the midst of the fighting there is excitement but the dominant emotion is fear. It is not easy to identify the good guys. To the Vietnamese, he may well be a bad guy. Close up the enemy looks a lot like ordinary people, some young men no older than Perry's brother Kenny. Readers are left to answer the "why are we here?" question for themselves.

Perry goes home knowing that he is no longer a child. As he and Peewee wait to board the plane home, they try to avoid noticing all the silver caskets that are going back with them. They have come almost full circle, but they have been forever changed. Perry learns that Judy Duncan, the nurse he had sat with on the flight to Vietnam, has been killed; the circle has been broken. As they stand in a tired and bedraggled line, a group of new recruits arrive, looking very much like the Perry and Peewee who landed in Vietnam months before. A new circle is beginning. Perry has become a different person, having learned "something about dying, and about trying to keep each other alive."

Fallen Angels is a powerful evocation of the Vietnam War and an indictment of war in general. It recognizes and celebrates the bonding that grows from shared experience. It also recognizes that young men who face the conditions of war also face themselves and find out what they are made of. Ultimately, though, it reminds us that, for the angel warriors—the boys we send off to fight before they have a chance to become men—war mostly provides lessons in how to kill in order to keep themselves from being killed. For many the lessons are not enough; they become the fallen angels. The survivors have other lessons to learn. Having learned to kill, having learned to face death, they come home to relearn what it means to be an ordinary human being.

6. The Present and the Future: Myers the Artist

Myers the Afro-American Novelist

One of Myers's major contributions has been his authentic and generally positive portrayal of Black life in urban United States. The significance of this contribution becomes clear when it is placed in its historical context. Myers's first book was published in 1969. Just four years earlier, Nancy Larrick had lamented in the pages of the *Saturday Review* the near-total absence of Blacks in books published by juvenile publishers between 1962 and 1964.[1] Historically, when Blacks had been portrayed in books for young people, the images presented had been laughable and insulting stereotypes, such as the servants in series like Tom Swift and the Bobbsey Twins. The advent of the civil rights movement of the sixties and the war on poverty of the Johnson administration, along with the generally liberal attitude in the country, stimulated a major increase in the numbers of books by and about Blacks and other so-called minorities.

During the early part of this period, books about Blacks were frequently written by white authors, and many suffered from a lack of authenticity. However, by 1975, when *Fast Sam* was published, Myers saw himself as a part of a new beginning. A number of young adult novels by Black authors had already been published. Kristin Hunter's *The Soul Brothers and Sister Lou* had won, in a different category, the same Council on Interracial Books for Children Minority Writers Contest that had given Myers his start. Other novels with urban settings were Sharon Bell Mathis's *Teacup Full of Roses* and *Listen for the Fig Tree*; June Jordan's *His Own Where*; Rosa Guy's *The Friends*; Eloise Greenfield's *Sister*; Alice Childress's *A Hero Ain't Nothin' but a Sandwich*. The year of *Fast Sam* was also the year that Virginia Hamilton became the first Black author to win the Newbery Medal, although it should be pointed out that *M. C. Higgins, the Great* was not an urban novel.

The urban novels of the late sixties and early seventies were part of the new realism in adolescent literature. They not only presented Black characters, but they included previously avoided topics such as drugs, sex, and street violence. The characters often lived in harsh circumstances, and the authors portrayed them realistically. Parents were not always positive role models, and endings were not always happy. Growing up Black in the city was shown to be a very difficult task.

Myers's contribution in his early books was to add a much needed touch of humor to the developing portrait of Black life in the city. Other Black authors were offering hope for overcoming adversity and focusing on the tradition of survival that is strong in the culture and an important theme in Afro-American novels. But Myers called attention to the laughter that is also a strong tradition and one of the tools for survival.

Although he is not unique in presenting authentic representations of Blacks and Black life, his is a unique voice. At this writing he is the only Black male currently and consistently publishing young adult novels. Although he shares certain aspects of his world view with Black women authors, his voice has been tuned by barbershops and street corners, bongo drums and fatherhood, basketball and military service. His brand of humor, his facile rendering of the rhetoric of Black teenage boys, his strong focus on fathers and sons, are all shaded by his experiences as a Black male. A look at Myers's urban novels reveals not only two sides of Black urban life, but also two important threads woven through the books. One thread is an authentic picture of life within a cultural group. The other is a set of themes, an offering of wisdom and insights into what it means to grow up a member of the Black community. In one set of his books, the harshness of the urban setting is backdrop; the focus is young people and their escapades. In the other, the urban setting is an integral part of the story itself. The portrayal of the Black experience and the insights he offers can be found in both.

The authenticity of Myers's portrayals of Black life is heightened by his weaving of important elements of Black culture into his stories. He is best known for his realistic representation of the rhetorical, grammatical, and semantic characteristics of Black English. Whenever his Black characters speak, they sound like real Black people. It should be noted that although his informal vernacular is most noticeable to critics, his characters reflect the full range of Black urban speech, both female and male, from street corner rapping to formal standard English.

Another cultural thread that Myers weaves through the urban novels is religion. Particularly in the novels that include older female characters (such as Grandma Carrie in *It Ain't All for Nothin'* and Sister Gibbs in *Crystal*) the language and the music of the Black church are used to build character and setting. On the other hand, particularly in *Mojo and the Russians*, Myers recognizes that non-Christian belief systems can still exist in the Black community side by side with Christianity.

Other aspects of Black culture are woven into the stories as a part of the setting, a reflection of the details of daily living of people who belong to a distinct cultural group. References to sacred and secular music and to musicians are sprinkled throughout the books. Aphorisms turn up frequently, often in the mouths of older women. Occasionally the names of a few Black heroes can be found. In one book, *The Legend of Tarik*, Myers offers to young Black readers an epic Black hero whose qualities—strength, determination, endurance, intelligence, compassion—represent a cultural ideal.

Myers himself identifies what he and the other Black novelists were doing: "I had learned from [Langston] Hughes that being a Black writer meant more than simply having one's characters brown-skinned, or having them live in what publishers insist on describing on book jackets as a 'ghetto.' It meant understanding the nuances of value, of religion, of dreams. It meant capturing the subtle rhythms of language and movement and weaving it all, the sound and the gesture, the sweat and the prayers, into the recognizable fabric of black life."[2]

Also woven into the tapestry of Black life that Myers offers his readers are insights that might help them understand what it means to grow up Black in the urban centers of this nation. Myers is clear about the obstacles and hardships that often must be faced in such a setting, especially by people who are poor. Drugs, gangs, and violence are a fact of life in many large cities. Social agencies cannot always be depended on to provide support, or if they do help, their support sometimes comes at the expense of a loss of pride, dignity, or control over one's own life. Racism is a given. Myers is also clear about the potential for overcoming the hardships. He writes of love and laughter and offers compassion and hope. He writes of the need to find strength within oneself and of the possibility of finding strength within the group, whether the group is the family, the peer group, or the community.

This notion of community support, of Blacks helping Blacks, is important to Myers. He notes that television programs and books by white authors often portray whites helping Blacks (as in "Different Strokes" or "Webster," in which white families adopt Black children), or they portray Blacks helping whites, whites helping whites, but not usually Blacks helping Blacks. Myers says, "I find that a very precious relationship, and it's being omitted, so when I write I thought I should write about that."

At the same time that his books offer insights about Black life, they also deal with themes that can be found in other young adult literature and in literature in general: friendships and peer relationships, family, individual and social responsibility, love, growing up, finding oneself. Myers succeeds, therefore, in embedding the universal inside the particulars of the reflected lives of people whose image, in the field of children's and young adult literature, had for too many years suffered neglect and abuse.

Again, Myers speaks for himself: "What I wanted to do was to portray this vital community as one that is very special to a lot of people. I wanted to show the people I knew as being as richly endowed with those universal traits of love, humor, ambition as any in the world. This, I hope, is what my books do. That space of earth was no ghetto, it was home. Those were not exotic stereotypes, those were my people. And I love them."[3]

Myers the Generalist

Myers is proud to be an Afro-American young adult novelist, but he is first of all a writer and can and does write about other people, in other genres, and about other topics. He has written short stories, nonfiction magazine pieces, nonfiction children's books, books for older elementary-age readers, mysteries, adventure stories, easy-to-read science fiction, picture books, and a new novel offering some blank space and invitations for the reader to add his or her own writing to the book.

The adult stories, published in the seventies, reveal some of Myers's versatility. The stories offer a different world view from that in his work for young people. There is some bitterness ("How Long Is Forever?"), tragedy ("The Vision of Felipe"), loneliness ("The Going On"), insanity ("The Dark Side of the Moon"). One or two may be precursors of the work to come. "The Vision of Felipe," set in Peru, features a gentle, sensitive, and compassionate young boy, who when orphaned by his grandmother's death goes off to the city to seek his fortune. Felipe is in many ways similar to Tito, the Puerto Rican boy in *Scorpions*. Like Tito, Felipe has been greatly influenced by his beloved grandmother's teachings, and his relationship with his friend Daniel is in some ways similar to that between Jamal and Tito. Other stories are related to Myers's young adult work only in that they explore similar topics. "Juby" includes a white person studying voodoo, though the story is in a much darker vein than *Mojo and the Russians*. The dialect used in the narrative has a Caribbean flavor

similar to the one in *Mr. Monkey and the Gotcha Bird*. Both
"Juby" and "Gums," in which a grandfather and his young grandson are overcome by their fear of a personified Death, may
have their roots in the scary stories Myers remembers his father
telling. "Bubba" features a white soldier who is part of the military
escort for the funeral of a Black soldier killed in Vietnam. He
spends the night in the home of the deceased soldier's mother
and has to confront the issue of racism as it sometimes operates
in the military. The issue is one of those touched on in *Fallen
Angels*.

Myers has also produced two nonfiction books for young people,
The World of Work and *Social Welfare*. *The World of Work* draws
on the knowledge Myers acquired when he was a vocational place-
ment supervisor for the New York State Employment Service. It
is a guide to selecting a career, including descriptions of numerous
jobs, their requirements, the method of entry, possibilities for
advancement. True to his storytelling self, Myers introduces *The
World of Work* with an imaginative speculation about how a hungry cave man might have created for himself the first job.

Social Welfare is a brief history and explanation of the welfare
system, how it operates, who it serves, its problems, and some
possible solutions. Both are well written—clear and straightfor-
ward. Both are over ten years old and somewhat dated, although
Social Welfare is not nearly as dated as its author might wish it
to be, given his expressed desire for change in the system. The
books are nonfiction that is accurate, clear, and interestingly written.

Myers is willing to take risks with format, genre, and style, and
he does so with varying degrees of success. *Brainstorm* is a science
fiction story written with a limited vocabulary and designed for
reluctant or remedial readers in fifth through eighth grades. Although Myers says that he would like to "bring some good literature" to the easy reader form, the restrictions on length and
vocabulary make that a difficult task. It *is* possible to do what he
did with *Brainstorm*—present interesting but undeveloped characters in a fast-moving plot. *Brainstorm* appeals also because it
uses black-and-white photographs of a diverse group of teenagers

who are the crew of a space ship sent to an alien planet to investigate the cause of a spate of "brainstorms" that have been destroying humans on earth.

Brainstorm received reasonably good notices, but the reviews of *The Black Pearl and the Ghost* range from scathingly negative to a cheerful acceptance of the book as spoof and a recognition of its good points. *Kirkus* called it "clunkingly obvious . . . hollow, creaky."[4] The *Children's Book Services* reviewer found it "static . . . neither well-written nor interesting . . . trivia."[5] On the other hand, *Booklist* saw "funny characters . . . sprightly pace,"[6] and *Horn Book* accepted it as "exaggerated in style and designed to meet the tastes of children."[7]

A good reviewer must consider what the author was trying to do. *The Black Pearl and the Ghost; or One Mystery after Another* is a spoof meant for children somewhere between ages seven and ten. The humor starts with the subtitle (the book consists of two mysteries, one after another) and continues through the joke shared with the reader but not the ghost-busting detective. It is a profusely illustrated book, although not quite a picture book, and an important part of the story is told in Robert Quackenbush's amusing pictures.

Myers's books for elementary school readers, including his picture books, show a vivid imagination at work. His realistic stories, *Where Does the Day Go?* and *The Dancers*, are built on premises that were unusual at the time of their publication: a group of Black and Hispanic children speculating about a natural phenomenon and receiving answers from a Black father, and a Black boy from Harlem intrigued by ballet. *Fly, Jimmy, Fly* shows a young boy using his imagination to soar above the city. *The Golden Serpent*, set in India and illustrated by the Provensens, sets up a mystery that it leaves unresolved. *The Dragon Takes a Wife* takes the traditional knight-fights-a-dragon tale and twists it to make the dragon the protagonist, as Kenneth Grahame did in *The Reluctant Dragon*. Then Myers adds a touch of Blackness in the form of Mabel Mae Jones and her hip, rhyming spells. Although *Kirkus* called it "intercultural hocus pocus,"[8] other reviewers found it amusing, even delightful. The imaginative humor works. *Mr. Monkey and the Gotcha Bird* dips into African and Caribbean folk traditions for its narrative voice and its trickster monkey who outsmarts the gotcha bird who would have him for supper.

Myers's novel for readers under twelve, *Me, Mop, and the Moondance Kid*, echoes some of the concerns and qualities of his young adult novels. The story is told by T.J., who, along with his younger brother, Moondance, has been recently adopted. Their task is to help their friend Mop (*Miss Olivia Parrish*), who is still at the orphanage, to be adopted too, preferably by the coach of their Little League team, which they are trying to turn into a winner. The style is typical Myers: T.J.'s narration is easygoing and humorous, characters are credible and likable, the plot moves along briskly, and the human relationships are warm.

Sweet Illusions is a young adult novel, published by the Teachers and Writers Collaborative, that experiments with format. It is an episodic novel focusing on teenage pregnancy. Not only is each chapter narrated by a different character, but at the end of each chapter the reader is invited to help create the story by writing a letter, a song, a list, a daydream. Lined pages are available for writing directly in the book (with a caution about not writing in library books). The characters are Black, white, and Hispanic, and all of them are learning of the difficulties and responsibilities involved in becoming parents. Both the young women and the fathers of their children tell their stories, which raise hard issues involved in teenage pregnancy: decisions about abortion and adoption, parental and community attitudes toward the mothers, irresponsibility on the part of the fathers, continuing their education, providing for the child. The book works. Myers has, in a brief space, managed to create believable characters with individual voices. Their stories are unique and at the same time recognizable to anyone who has thought about or grappled with the problems of teenage pregnancy. The purpose is to provoke thought, which happens as readers get caught up in the characters and their stories.

In spite of its workbook format, *Sweet Illusions* received some serious critical attention. *Booklist*, for example, gave it high praise, calling it "an astute, realistic consideration of some of the problems associated with teenage pregnancy, valuable for personal reading as well as classroom discussion." Further, the reviewer found that "Myers' profiles are quick and clever; his characters, stubborn, confused, and vulnerable, draw substance and individuality from tough, savvy dialogue and credible backdrops."[9] It is an unusual book that succeeds because it draws on Myers's highly developed craftsmanship.

The Myers Craft

Myers has developed a number of strengths as a writer. Critics agree that he has a fine ear for dialogue, which becomes one of the major means he uses to develop characterization and authenticate settings. Partly because their speech seems real, his characters seem real, too. Myers approaches his characters with warmth and sensitivity; he understands the concerns of young people. His first-person narratives project an intimacy that invites readers immediately into the world of the protagonist. Once there, his flair for drama keeps the pages turning.

When he wants to write humor, he knows how to create it with characterization, with language play, and with situations. Even in his serious books, humor is sometimes interjected, as in the scene in which a Hari Krishna and a Black Muslim fight over saving Tippy's soul in the bus station in *It Ain't All for Nothin'*. When the focus of a Myers book is humor, as in *Mojo and the Russians*, a reader may often laugh out loud.

Critics have not paid much attention to Myers's ability to turn a phrase, to create sharp, clear images outside the context of dialogue, but some of his figurative language is particularly apt. In *Won't Know*, he describes the house the seniors live in as seeming to "squat in the middle of the block, . . . thinking of itself as slightly better than the rest. It gave you the feeling that if it had been human it would have been a fat old man who used to have a lot of money." *Fallen Angels* is replete with vivid figurative language that brings to life the experience of war.

As has been pointed out in the discussion of the novels, critics are not unanimous in their praise of Myers's work. Reviewers who have found flaws in his craft have focused on three areas: credibility (e.g., *Mojo and the Russians, The Young Landlords, The Nicholas Factor*), unevenness in plot (e.g., *Won't Know Till I Get There, Crystal, Hoops, The Legend of Tarik*), and weak characterization (e.g., *The Nicholas Factor, The Legend of Tarik*). These assessments are not unanimous, however: for every reviewer who found one of those aspects flawed, another found it strong.

The charges of lack of credibility occur in his humorous novels and in the adventure stories and can be answered by examining Myers's style and the genre in which he is writing. In his humorous novels, some critics respond to the exaggeration that is a part of a Black rhetorical style by testing the escapades of the young people against reality and finding them unbelievable. The adventure stories, too, employ some exaggeration, which may displease some reviewers.

Some of the urban novels, such as *Won't Know Till I Get There* and *Hoops*, have been described as slow moving. This unevenness may also be attributed to an aspect of Black rhetorical style, narrative sequencing, in which there is a tendency to meander off the route to the point one is trying to make, to take the long way when the direct route would be quicker.[10]

The accusation of weak characterization came in response to *The Nicolas Factor* and *The Legend of Tarik*, both of which incorporate enough of the elements of the romantic adventure novel to influence the character development in the direction of types. Ironically, Myers has also been praised for his ability to create credible, well-delineated characters.

Myers's strengths as a novelist far outweigh his occasional shortcomings. In the *Horn Book* review of *Fallen Angels*, Ethel Heins referred to Myers as "a writer of skill, judgment, and maturity."[11] He has honed that skill on a set of books that have earned him a place as one of the most important writers of young adult literature in the country today.

The Future

Myers loves his work. He seems always to be juggling a number of different projects—a book on Black history, a fictional book about a singer who moves from the church to secular music, another book on the order of *Sweet Illusions*, another picture book, even a book of nursery rhymes. "As a writer there are many issues I would like to tackle. I am interested in loneliness, in our attempts to escape reality through the use of drugs or through our own psychological machinations. I am interested in how we deal with each other, both sexually and in other ways, and the reasons we so often reject each other."[12]

He has achieved some status in the field and is eager to stretch, to explore any and all kinds of ideas, to break away from whatever restrictions seem to be imposed on him because he is a Black writer. At the same time, he will continue writing about the lives of ordinary Black people, "to tell Black children about their humanity and about their history and how to grease their legs so the ash won't show and how to braid their hair so it's easy to comb on frosty winter mornings."[13] May he keep on keepin' on; it ain't all for nothin'.

APPENDIX

Honors and Awards Won by
Walter Dean Myers

Fallen Angels

- American Library Association Best Book for Young Adults
- Notable Children's Trade Book in the Social Studies
- Coretta Scott King Award

Fast Sam, Cool Clyde, and Stuff

- American Library Association Notable Book

Hoops

- American Library Association Best Book for Young Adults

It Ain't All for Nothin'

- American Library Association Notable Book

The Legend of Tarik

- American Library Association Best Book for Young Adults
- Notable Children's Trade Book in the Social Studies

Motown and Didi

- Coretta Scott King Award

Scorpions

- Newbery Honor Book
- American Library Association Best Book for Young Adults

The Young Landlords

- American Library Association Notable Book
- American Library Association Best Book for Young Adults
- Coretta Scott King Award

Where Does the Day Go?

- Council on Interracial Books for Children Award

Notes and References

1. Literature As Liberation: The Making of a Writer

1. Writers' Program of the Works Project Administration in the State of West Virginia, *West Virginia: A Guide to the Mountain State* (New York: Oxford University Press, 1941), 303.

2. *Something about the Author Autobiography Series*, vol. 2. ed. Adele Sarkissian (Detroit: Gale Research Co., 1986), 144.

3. "The Young Adult Novel: Writing for Aliens," speech presented at the breakfast meeting of the Adolescent Literature Assembly, seventy-eighth annual convention of the National Council of Teachers of English, 19 November 1988, St. Louis, Missouri.

4. *Something about the Author Autobiography Series*, 145.

5. NCTE speech.

6. Ibid.

7. *Something about the Author Autobiography Series*, 146.

8. Ibid., 145.

9. Ibid., 148.

10. Ibid., 148.

11. NCTE speech.

12. *Something about the Author Autobiography Series*, 149.

13. Ibid., 152.

14. Ibid., 153.

15. "The Black Experience in Children's Books: One Step Forward, Two Steps Back." *Interracial Books for Children Bulletin* 10, no.6 (1979): 15.

16. *Something about the Author Autobiography Series*. 155.

17. NCTE speech.

18. Ibid.

2. With Love and Laughter: Myers the Humorist

1. Zora Neal Hurston, "High John de Conquer," in *The Book of Negro Folklore*, ed. Langston Hughes and Arna Bontemps (New York: Dodd, Mead, 1958), 95.

2. Review of *Fast Sam, Cool Clyde, and Stuff, Horn Book* (August 1975): 388–89.

3. Robert Lipsyte, review of *Fast Sam, New York Times Book Review*, 4 May 1975, 28–29.

4. Review of *Fast Sam, Booklist* (15 February 1975): 620.

5. *Something about the Author Autobiography Series*, 151.

6. Review of *Mojo and the Russians, Bulletin of the Center for Children's Books* (April 1978): 132.

7. Robert Unsworth, review of *Mojo and the Russians, School Library Journal* (November 1977): 74.

8. Patricia Lee Gauch, review of *The Young Landlords, New York Times Book Review*, 6 January 1980. 20.

9. Ibid.

10. Review of *The Young Landlords, Kirkus Reviews* (15 January 1980): 70–71.

11. Review of *The Young Landlords, Booklist* (1 December 1979): 560.

12. Review of *Won't Know Till I Get There, Publishers Weekly* (4 June 1982): 67.

13. Hazel Rochman, review of *Won't Know Till I Get There, School Library Journal* (May 1982): 72–73.

14. Geneva Smitherman, *Talkin and Testifyin: The Language of Black America* (Boston: Houghton Mifflin, 1977), 35–166.

15. Ibid., 118.

16. Ibid., 121.

17. Ibid., 131.

18. Ibid., 132.

19. Ibid., 100, 134.

20. Ibid., 104.

21. Ibid., 79.

22. Ibid., 94.

23. Ibid., 42, 43.

24. Ibid., 58.

3. On Compassion and Hope: Myers the Realist

1. Langston Hughes. "Harlem," in *The Panther and the Lash: Poems of Our Times* (New York: Knopf, 1969), 4.

2. Bernard W. Bell. *The Afro-American Novel and Its Tradition* (Amherst: University of Massachusetts Press, 1987), 342.

3. Steven Matthews, review of *It Ain't All for Nothin'*, *School Library Journal* (October 1978): 158.

4. Jeanne Betancourt, review of *Crystal, New York Times Book Review*, 13 September 1987. 48.

5. Review of *Motown and Didi*, *Publishers Weekly* (26 October 1984): 105.

6. Review of *It Ain't All for Nothin'*, *Bulletin of the Center for Children's Books* (January 1979): 84–85.

7. Review of *Crystal, Bulletin of the Center for Children's Books* (June 1987): 71.

8. Review of *Motown and Didi*, *Bulletin of the Center for Children's Books* (January 1985): 90.

9. Review of *Scorpions, Horn Book* (July–August 1988): 504.

10. Review of *Hoops, Booklist* (15 September 1981): 98.

11. Matthews, review of *It Ain't All for Nothin'*, 158.

12. Review of *Crystal, Booklist* (1 June 1987): 1516.

13. Betancourt, review of *Crystal*, 48.

14. Review of *Crystal, Publishers Weekly* (8 May 1987): 71.

15. Review of *Hoops, Booklist*, 98.

16. Review of *Outside Shot, Booklist* (15 October 1984): 300.

17. Review of *Outside Shot, Bulletin of the Center for Children's Books* (January 1985): 90–91.

18. Review of *It Ain't All for Nothin'*, *Booklist* (September 1970): 40.

19. Review of *Scorpions, Bulletin of the Center for Children's Books* (June 1988): 235.

20. Review of *Scorpions, Horn Book* (July–August 1988): 504.

4. Of Mystery and Adventure: Myers the Storyteller

1. Review of *The Nicholas Factor, Publishers Weekly* (18 March 1983): 70.

2. Review of *The Nicholas Factor, Bulletin of the Center for Children's Books* (July–August 1983): 214.

3. Lucy V. Hawley, review of *The Nicholas Factor, School Library Journal* (September 1983): 138.

4. Review of *The Nicholas Factor, Kirkus Reviews* (15 June 1983): 665.

5. Review of *The Nicholas Factor, Horn Book* (June 1983): 314–15.

6. Review of *The Legend of Tarik, Booklist* (15 July 1981): 1449.

7. Ethel Twichell, review of *The Legend of Tarik, Horn Book* (August 1981): 434.

8. Hazel Rochman, review of *The Legend of Tarik, School Library Journal* (May 1981): 76.

9. Alex Boyd, review of *The Legend of Tarik, Voice of Youth Advocates* (October 1981): 36.

10. Review of *The Legend of Tarik, Booklist,* 1449.

11. Malcolm Bosse, review of *The Legend of Tarik, New York Times Book Review,* 12 July 1981, 30.

12. Ibid.

13. Ethel Twichell, review of *The Legend of Tarik,* 434.

5. Of Battles and Brotherhood: Myers the War Novelist

1. Mel Watkins, review of *Fallen Angels, New York Times Book Review,* 22 January 1989, 29.

2. Maria B. Salvatore, review of *Fallen Angels, School Library Journal* (June–July 1988): 118.

3. Ethel Heins, review of *Fallen Angels, Horn Book* (July–August 1988): 503.

4. Watkins, review of *Fallen Angels,* 29.

6. The Present and the Future: Myers the Artist

1. Nancy Larrick, "The All-White World of Children's Books. *Saturday Review* (September 1965): 63–65, 84–85.

2. "I Actually Thought We Would Revolutionize the Industry," *New York Times Book Review,* 9 November 1986, 50.

3. *The Fifth Book of Junior Authors and Illustrators,* ed. Sally Holmes Holtze (New York: Wilson, 1983), 226.

4. Review of *The Black Pearl and the Ghost, Kirkus Reviews* (April 1980): 514.

5. Review of *The Black Pearl and the Ghost, Children's Book Review Service* (Spring 1980): 113.

6. Review of *The Black Pearl and the Ghost, Booklist* (1 May 1980): 1297.

7. Review of *The Black Pearl and the Ghost, Horn Book* (June 1980): 301–02.

8. Review of *The Dragon Takes a Wife, Kirkus Reviews* (1 March 1972): 256.

9. Review of *Sweet Illusions, Booklist* (15 June 1987): 1591.

10. Geneva Smitherman, *Talkin and Testifyin: The Language of Black America* (Boston: Houghton Mifflin, 1977), 161.

11. Ethel Heins, review of *Fallen Angels, Horn Book* (July–August 1988): 503.

12. *Something about the Author Autobiographical Series*, 155.

13. Ibid.

Selected Bibliography

Primary Works

Novels

Adventure in Granada. New York: Viking Puffin, 1985.
Ambush in the Amazon. New York: Viking Puffin, 1986.
Brainstorm (photographs by Chuck Freedman). New York: Franklin Watts, 1977; Dell, 1979.
Crystal. New York: Viking, 1987.
Duel in the Desert. New York: Viking Puffin. 1986.
Fallen Angels. New York: Scholastic, 1988.
Fast Sam, Cool Clyde, and Stuff. New York: Viking, 1975: Avon, 1978; Penguin, 1988.
The Hidden Shrine. New York: Viking Puffin, 1985.
Hoops. New York: Delacorte, 1981; Dell, 1983.
It Ain't All for Nothin'. New York: Viking, 1978; Avon, 1985.
The Legend of Tarik. New York: Viking, 1981; Scholastic, 1982.
Me, Mop, and the Moondance Kid. New York: Delacorte, 1988.
Mojo and the Russians. New York: Viking, 1977; Avon, 1979.
Motown and Didi. New York: Viking, 1984.
The Nicholas Factor. New York: Viking, 1983.
The Outside Shot. New York: Delacorte, 1984; Dell, 1987.
Scorpions. New York: Harper, 1988.
Sweet Illusions. New York: Teachers and Writers Collaborative, 1986.
Tales of a Dead King. New York: Morrow, 1983.
Won't Know Till I Get There. New York: Viking, 1982; Penguin 1988.
The Young Landlords. New York: Viking, 1979.

Picture Books

The Black Pearl and the Ghost; or, One Mystery after Another (illustrated by Robert Quackenbush). New York: Viking. 1980.
The Dancers (illustrated by Anne Rockwell). New York: Parents Magazine Press, 1969.
The Dragon Takes a Wife (illustrated by Ann Grifalconi). Indianapolis: Bobbs-Merrill, 1972.
Fly, Jimmy, Fly (illustrated by Moneta Barnett). New York: Putnam, 1974.
The Golden Serpent (illustrated by Alice and Martin Provensen). New York: Viking, 1980.
Mr. Monkey and the Gotcha Bird (illustrated by Leslie Morrill). New York: Delacorte, 1984.
Where Does the Day Go? (illustrated by Leo Carty). New York: Parents Magazine Press, 1969.

Nonfiction

Social Welfare. New York: Franklin Watts, 1976.
The World of Work: A Guide to Choosing a Career. Indianapolis: Bobbs-Merrill, 1975.

Short Stories

"Bubba." *Essence*, November 1972, 56, 74, 76.
"Dark Side of the Moon." *Black Creation*, Fall 1971, 26–29.
"The Fare to Crown Point." In *What We Must See: Young Black Storytellers*, edited by Orde Coombs, 113–27. New York: Dodd, Mead, 1971.
"The Going On." *Black World*, March 1971, 61–67.
"Gums." In *We Be Word Sorcerers*, edited by Sonia Sanchez, 181–188. New York: Bantam, 1973.
"How Long Is Forever?" *Negro Digest*, June 1969, 52–57.
"Juby." *Black Creation*, April 1971, 26–27.
"The Vision of Felipe." *The Black Scholar*, November–December 1978, 2–9.

Articles

"The Black Experience in Children's Books: One Step Forward, Two Steps Back." *Interracial Books for Children Bulletin* 10, no. 6 (1979): 14–15.

"Gifts." *Horn Book* 62 (July–August 1986): 436–37.

"I Actually Thought We Would Revolutionize the Industry." *New York Times Book Review*, 9 November 1986, 50.

Something about the Author Autobiography Series. Edited by Adele Sarkissian. vol. 2, 143–56. Detroit: Gale Research Co., 1986.

Speech

"The Young Adult Novel: Writing for Aliens." Speech presented at the meeting of the Adolescent Literature Assembly, seventy-eighth annual convention of the National Council of Teachers of English, St. Louis, Missouri, November 1988. Cassette recording.

Secondary Works

Books and Parts of Books

Bell, Bernard W. *The Afro-American Novel and Its Tradition.* Amherst: University of Massachusetts Press, 1987.

Commire, Anne, ed. *Something about the Author.* Vol. 41. Detroit: Gale Research Co., 1985.

Davis, Thadious M., and Trudier Harris, eds. *Afro-American Fiction Writers after 1955.* Dictionary of Literary Biography, vol. 33. Detroit: Gale Research Co., 1984.

Donelson, Kenneth L., and Alleen Pace Nilsen. *Literature for Today's Young Adults.* 3d ed. Glenview, Ill.: Scott, Foresman, 1989.

Gates, Henry Louis, Jr. *The Signifying Monkey: A Theory of Afro-American Literary Criticism.* New York: Oxford University Press, 1988.

Holtze, Sally H., ed. *Fifth Book of Junior Authors and Illustrators.* New York: Wilson, 1983.

Lukens, Rebecca J. *A Critical Handbook of Children's Literature.* Glenview, Ill.: Scott, Foresman, 1982.

Marowski, Daniel G., ed. *Contemporary Literary Criticism.* Vol. 35. Detroit: Gale Research Co., 1985.

Metzger, Linda, and Deborah Straub, eds. *Contemporary Authors, New Revision Series.* Vol. 20. Detroit: Gale Research Co., 1987.

Sloan, Glenna Davis. *The Child as Critic: Teaching Literature in Elementary and Middle Schools.* 2d ed. New York: Teachers College Press, 1984.

Smitherman, Geneva. *Talkin and Testifyin: The Language of Black America.* Boston: Houghton Mifflin, 1977.

Article

Wideman, John Edgar. "The Black Writer and the Magic of the Word." *New York Times Book Review,* 24 January 1988, 1, 28–29.

Book Reviews

The Black Pearl and the Ghost
Booklist, 1 May 1980, 1297.
Children's Book Review Service, Spring 1980, 113.
Horn Book, June 1980, 301–2.
Kirkus Reviews, April 1980, 514.

Brainstorm
Manning, Patricia. *School Library Journal,* November 1977, 60.

Crystal
Booklist, 1 June 1987, 1516.
Bulletin of the Center for Children's Books, May 1987, 175.
New York Times Book Review, 13 September 1987, 48.
Publishers Weekly, 8 May 1987, 71.

The Dancers
Bulletin of the Center for Children's Books, July–August 1972, 174.
Lapidus, Hilda. *Library Journal,* September 1972, 2940.

The Dragon Takes a Wife
Bulletin of the Center for Children's Books, December 1972, 61–62.
Griffin, Nancy. *New York Times Book Review,* 9 April 1972, 8.
Kirkus Reviews, 1 March 1972, 256.

Fallen Angels
Campbell, Patty. *Wilson Library Bulletin,* March 1988, 76.
Heins, Ethel. *Horn Book,* July–August 1988, 503.

Salvatore, Maria B. *School Library Journal*, June–July 1988, 118.
Watkins, Mel. *New York Times Book Review*, 22 January 1989, 29.

Fast Sam, Cool Clyde, and Stuff
Bulletin of the Center for Children's Books, January 1976, 82–83.
Horn Book, August 1975, 388–89.
Lipsyte, Robert. *New York Times Book Review*, 4 May 1975, 28–29.
Spence, Patricia Anne. *Interracial Books for Children Bulletin*, vol. 6, no. 8 (1975): 5.

The Golden Serpent
Booklist 15 December 1980, 575.
Bulletin of the Center for Children's Books, April 1981, 157.
Horn Book, December 1980, 636.
Warwick, Ellen D. *School Library Journal*, January 1981, 53.

Hoops
Booklist, 15 September 1981, 98.
Bulletin of the Center for Children's Books, December 1981, 74.
Martin, Ruth. *Best Sellers*, February 1982, 442–43.

It Ain't All for Nothin'
Booklist, September 1978, 40.
Bulletin of the Center for Children's Books, January 1979, 84–85.
Horn Book, October 1978, 518–19.
Kirkus Reviews, October 1978, 1143.
Pennington, Jane. *Interracial Books for Children Bulletin*, vol. 10, no. 4 (1979): 18.

The Legend of Tarik
Booklist, 15 July 1981, 1449.
Bosse, Malcolm. *New York Times Book Review*, 12 July 1981, 30.
Rochman, Hazel. *School Library Journal*, May 1981, 76.
Twichell, Ethel R. *Horn Book*, August 1981, 434.

Mr. Monkey and the Gotcha Bird
Booklist, 15 February 1985, 847–48.
Publishers Weekly, 21 December 1984, 87–88.
Williams, Helen E. *School Library Journal*, January 1985, 66.

Mojo and the Russians
Booklist, 15 October 1977, 379.
Bulletin of the Center for Children's Books, April 1978, 132.
Unsworth, Robert. *School Library Journal*, November 1977, 74.

Motown and Didi
Horn Book, March–April 1985, 186–87.
Jackson, Gale. *School Library Journal*, March 1985, 180–81.
Publishers Weekly, 26 October 1984, 105.

The Nicholas Factor
Bulletin of the Center for Children's Books, July–August 1983, 214.
Hawley, Lucy V. *School Library Journal*, September 1983, 138.
Horn Book, June 1983, 314–15.
Morgans, Patricia A. *Best Sellers*, July 1983, 155.
Xavier, Becky Johnson. *Voice of Youth Advocates*, December 1983, 279–80.

The Outside Shot
Booklist, 15 October 1984, 300.
Bulletin of the Center for Children's Books, January 1985, 91.
Caywood, Carolyn. *School Library Journal*, November 1984, 135–36.

Scorpions
Bulletin of the Center for Children's Books, June 1988, 235.
Horn Book, July–August 1988, 504.
School Library Journal, September 1988, 201.

Sweet Illusions
Booklist, 15 June 1987, 1591.
Kirkus Reviews, February 1987, 228.
Moore, Virginia B. *Voice of Youth Advocates*, August 1987, 122.

Tales of a Dead King
Booklist, 1 January 1984, 683.
Kirkus Reviews, November 1983, 205.
School Library Journal, December 1983, 83.

Where Does the Day Go?
Bulletin of the Center for Children's Books, May 1970, 148.
Eble, Mary. *Library Journal*, 15 April 1970, 1629.

Won't Know Till I Get There
Booklist, 1 June 1982, 1315.
Edelman, Diane G. "Children's Books". *New York Times Book Review*, 13 June 1982, 26–27.
Horn Book, August 1982, 415–16.
Rochman, Hazel. *School Library Journal*, May 1982, 72–73.

The Young Landlords
Booklist, 1 December 1979, 560.
Gaugh, Patricia L. "Children's Books". *New York Times Book Review*, 6 January 1980, 20.
Horn Book, October 1978, 535.
Kirkus Reviews, 15 January 1980, 70–71.
Pennington, Ashley J. *Interracial Books for Children Bulletin*, vol. 12, no. 1 (1981): 15.

Index

About the Author

Rudine Sims Bishop is professor of education at The Ohio State University, where she teaches courses in children's literature in teacher education programs. She is author of *Shadow and Substance: Afro-American Experience in Contemporary Children's Literature* and several articles, reviews, and chapters on literature and literacy. Active in the National Council of Teachers of English, she is a former chair of the Elementary Section Committee and member of the Executive Committee. She currently serves as chair of NCTE's Children's Literature Assembly. She is a member of the staff of *The Web*, an Ohio State periodical committed to presenting to teachers "*wonderfully exciting books*" to use in their classrooms. Bishop lives in Columbus with her husband, Jim, and their springer spaniel, Barney.